1000
LIFE HACKS

1000
LIFE HACKS

Clever ways to make your life easier at home, work, and play

Dan Grabham

METRO BOOKS
New York

METRO BOOKS
New York

An Imprint of Sterling Publishing
387 Park Avenue South
New York, NY 10016

**First edition for the United States
and Canada published in 2016
by Metro Books**

**A QUINTET BOOK
Copyright © 2016
Quintet Publishing Limited**

**All rights reserved. No part of this
publication may be reproduced, stored
in a retrieval system, or transmitted in
any form or by any means (including
electronic, mechanical, photocopying,
recording, or otherwise) without prior
written permission from
the publisher.**

ISBN: 978-1-4351-6244-0

QTT.1LHK

**Conceived, designed
and produced by:
Quintet Publishing
4th Floor, Ovest House
58 West Street
Brighton BN1 2RA
United Kingdom**

**Project Editor: Rica Dearman
Designer: Bonnie Bryan
Photographer: Brent Darby
Art Director: Michael Charles
Senior Editor: Caroline Elliker
Publisher: Mark Searle**

Manufactured in China by Toppan Leefung
Printing Ltd.

2 4 6 8 10 9 7 5 3 1

Contents

Introduction

Time is increasingly precious for us all, so why not make the very most of it? More and more of us are looking for ways to improve how we tick off the tasks of life, whether that is saving time, money, or just doing things better. This book is the ultimate collection of inspired hints, tips, and advice for doing things more quickly, and more efficiently.

Life hacks are tips, shortcuts, or improvised methods for doing things better; whether that's to save time, save money, or be more productive. In this book you'll find a plethora of tricks, shortcuts, skills, and ingenious solutions to everyday problems.

While there's plenty here involving rubber bands, vinegar, baking soda, and safety pins, it's not all make and mend; life hacks are also little pieces of general improvement advice. We've done our best to pick out life guidance over the eight chapters of this book, including things like office politics, parenting teens, keeping fit, and making sure you don't fall foul of the fashion police.

The key idea is that life hacks not only help you get things done, they help you do things in a better way than you would have done otherwise.

One criticism of the more practical life hacks is that it sometimes takes too much time to carry them out—time you could have spent doing other things. At times that's true, but many of the things we've talked about in this book aren't just one-offs—the tips will come in useful again and again.

"Hacks" are, essentially, workarounds or shortcuts to solve problems, and the word has extended to include advice and tips on the issues of life. The term "life hack" (and the movement of "life hacking") has been around for approximately a decade, and originated in the U.S., where it was first used to describe the shortcuts taken by I.T. workers to get tasks completed. The term gained popularity through a magazine column and several websites.

When putting together this book, we intended for it to have something for everyone, and although some hacks are more specific in their target audience, many of the tips can be taken on by absolutely anybody, whether office worker, retiree, college student, or homeworker.

Group your hair-styling accessories

A piece of drainpipe makes a great holder for your hairdryer or curling tongs, especially if you can hide it between a piece of furniture and the wall.

There are many areas in life in which hacks can help. We have included hacks for the following:

Tech and workplace hacks

Many of us spend a significant part of our lives at work, and technology can be an important part of our jobs. Indeed, it also plays a major role in our everyday lives. But technology shouldn't be a frustration, and there's no reason why you can't make it work better for you. In this chapter we've gathered together ways you can get more from your smartphone, tablet, laptop, or desktop computer. We also show you how you can be more efficient in your work, and provide some top ergonomic tips for being more comfortable when at work.

Home and cleaning hacks

Keeping your home clean and efficient requires some out-of-the-box thinking and using materials you might not expect—they all work, though! Learn how to clear up grease, grass stains, cloudy headlights, clogged showerheads, and more. We tell you how to get stains out of carpets (as well as pet hair and furniture dents), and how to revitalize an old couch. We also give you a complete guide to baking soda—the best home-cleaning product you never knew you had.

DIY hacks

DIY can be a pain, but it doesn't need to be—here are some cunning fixes to common problems, and clever ways to store your stuff. Slipping rug? We've got you covered. Stripped screw? No problem. Need to find your key in the dark? Sorted. We've also included plenty of tips for painting your home efficiently and minimizing mess, as well as hints for gardening and greenhouses (if you're into that). We also have some really clever uses for coffee grounds, plus a bunch of great DIY car hacks for storage, running repairs, and de-icing.

Fashion hacks

Our clothing and fashion tips feature a bunch of methods you can use to repair and refresh the clothes you have so you'll always look your best. There's also a whole heap of tips if you're going out to buy a special outfit, as well as clothing storage, fashion dos and don'ts, and practical advice about looking after shoes and boots. We've plenty of stain-removal and clothes-cleaning tips, too. Finally, we have brilliant makeup tips and tricks, and plenty of uses for one of the greatest substances on the planet—petroleum jelly.

Food hacks

There's a whole host of ingenious ways to better organize and prepare food and drinks without breaking the bank with new equipment. We have plenty of tips, whatever your experience in the kitchen, including fresh new ways to enjoy food. There are also plenty of great ways to work with common kitchen items in a host of new and interesting ways, as well as ingenious methods for cooking staples, such as eggs. We'll tell you how to cut cake layers horizontally, keep salad fresh, revive celery, ripen bananas, make interesting pancakes, and slice mushrooms in an instant. Lastly, there are tips on eating more healthily, and satisfying your hunger at work.

Fitness hacks

We'd all like to exercise more. Here's how to stay healthier and make time for more exercise, as well as how you can make the most of the workouts you already do. We have great tips for beginners going to the gym or starting to run, and helpful hints on burning calories, swimming, fitness regimes, gym etiquette, and much more. We also have tips on how to plan your exercise (and not avoid it), and how to get better sleep.

Brighten up outfits with accessories

Remember that accessories can give a drab outfit a new lease of life or burst of color. Scarves are especially good.

The life of running shoes

The shock absorbency of running shoes does wear out—but how quickly depends on how much you run. A good rule of thumb is to change them every 400 to 500 miles of use.

Travel hacks

There are plenty of ways you can be shrewd while traveling—making the most of your money and time, and giving yourself a better experience in hotels, in the air, and at airports. There are plenty of helpful hints on packing, backpacking, business travel, dealing with liquid restrictions, pickpockets, and what to do when you're away. How much should you plan long breaks? We've also got special sections on how to improve the experience of flying, as well as how to deal with the minefield of traveling with colleagues!

Kids and parenting

Babies. Toddlers. Teenagers. All have their own challenges, many created by parents. We run you through advice on being generally less hassled as a parent, including tips on feeding, talking more positively, family time, making rules, storing the masses of toys you have/will have, and—yes—dealing with other parents who are all too keen to tell you what you should do. Finally, we talk teenagers, including money tips and curfews, before covering ideas for dealing with the thorny issue of kids and technology.

After all that, we hope you agree that getting into life hacks is addictive—in no time at all you'll be wondering how you managed without the new tricks you've adopted. Enjoy living a more efficient life!

1

WORK AND TECH

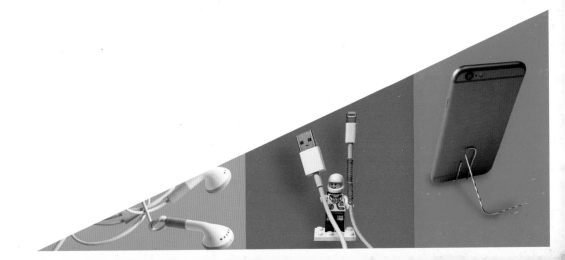

1> If you have family or business contacts in different time zones, it can be really handy to see what time it is where they are before calling them. So why not add more clocks to your computer desktop? On a PC, right-click on the clock in the bottom right of the screen (called the notifications area). Choose Adjust Date/Time from the menu. Choose the Additional Clocks tab and adjust the settings there to suit. On OS X you will need an extra app, such as Clocks from the Mac App Store.

2> Use a secure password that's a random collection of letters and numbers. It sounds simple—but how many of us have passwords that aren't very hard to guess?

3> Get dictionary definitions from Google by typing "define [word]" into the search engine or the browser's address bar.

4> If you have a folder of files you always use, online cloud storage is the way forward. You can synchronize the folder between all of your computers and access those same files on your cell phone.

5> Got a new PC? Ninite (www.ninite.com) is your answer. It enables you to select the browsers, media players, utilities, and anti-virus software you want to use, and install it all in one big bundle. This will save you hours. If you have a Mac, Get Mac Apps (www.getmacapps.com) is where you should go.

6> Want to know if your plane has left its previous destination on time? Or find out if your partner will arrive at the airport on schedule? Check out FlightAware for iOS and Android, and online at www.flightaware.com.

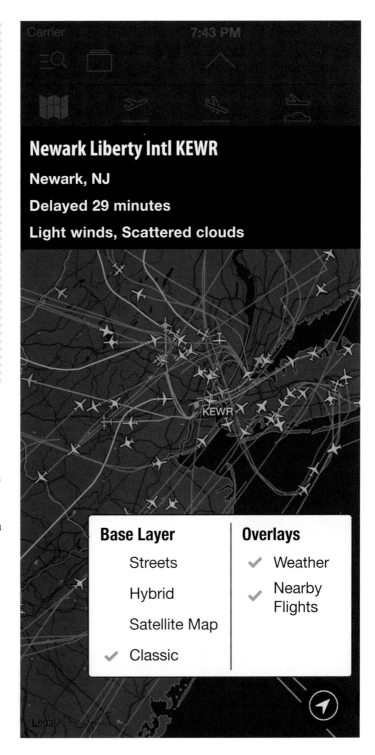

20 brilliant **iOS** tips and tricks

Pay Your wallet. Without the wallet.

7> To get to Apple Pay, double-click the Home button. You can toggle the double-click feature on and off in Settings > Wallet & Apple Pay.

8> Save battery life with the new Low Power Mode in the latest version of the iPhone software—iOS 9. Switch this on in Settings > Battery > Low Power Mode, and you'll be asked if you want to turn it on when you have 10 percent of your battery life remaining.

9> You can also now look at which apps use the most battery power. Again, you can access this in Settings > Battery.

10> In iOS 9, there's a new back button in the top left-hand corner.

11> If you find the capital letters on the keyboard confusing, it's easy to ask your iPhone or iPad to display lowercase letters when the shift or caps lock keys aren't in action—in Settings > Accessibility > Keyboard, toggle Show Lowercase Keys to on.

12> Looking for a contact? You can now call, message, or FaceTime someone directly from the search results. Just tap the icon you want on the screen. You can also use the search feature to perform quick calculations or check out the day's forecast—just type in "weather." Or you can always ask Siri, your iPhone's digital assistant, of course.

13> If you have problems with poor Wi-Fi, use Wi-Fi Assist. Your iPhone will then use your cellular data connection whenever Wi-Fi is poor. Go to Settings > Cellular > Wi-Fi Assist (it's further down the screen).

14> Siri can be silenced when your phone is set to silent—and so it should. In Settings > General > Siri > Voice Feedback, choose Control with Ring Switch.

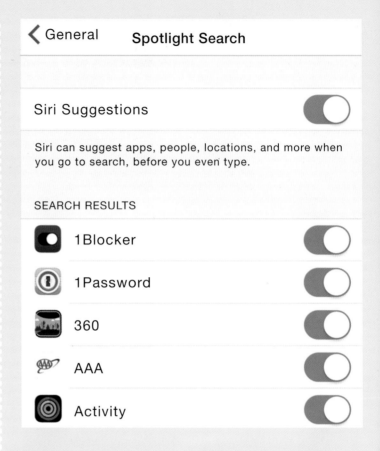

General   Spotlight Search

Siri Suggestions

Siri can suggest apps, people, locations, and more when you go to search, before you even type.

SEARCH RESULTS

1Blocker

1Password

360

AAA

Activity

15> If you use Siri, you can now ask it to "remind me about this tomorrow at 12pm." Your phone will then remind you about whatever you were viewing at that point.

16> You can ask Siri to find photos from a specific time or location, which is pretty handy. It uses the groupings that are automatically shown in the Photos app, so you don't have to manually tag.

17> The iOS search feature (called Spotlight) now enables you to search properly within apps—but you may not want this feature for all apps. In Settings > General > Spotlight Search, toggle off the apps you don't want.

18> The latest version of the Notes app enables you to scribble simple notes with your finger. You can draw with a marker, pen, or pencil. You're also now able to create to-do lists with checkboxes as well as add photos and links.

19> If you want to zoom in on part of a video, you can pinch-to-zoom, just as you can on a photo in iOS 9.

20> You can search for a word or phrase in the Safari browser. Just tap the Share icon and then tap Find on Page.

21> Select multiple photos in the Photos app by tapping Select, pressing on a photo, and then dragging down and left or right across multiple images to select them. You can also now swipe downward from the center of the screen to get back to the camera.

22> If you tap the search bar in Apple Maps you now get common searches to use. You have a few options—Food, Drinks, Shopping, Travel (local highlights), Services (like banks), Fun (like movie theaters), Health (local hospitals), and Transport (local stations).

23> To restrict the types of access people can have to your device, go to Restrictions:

1. Go to Settings > General > Restrictions.

2. Choose to Enable Restrictions.

3. Choose what you want to disallow, such as access to the camera, the ability to install apps, or buy in-app purchases.

24> Change the quality of the video your iPhone shoots—go to Settings > Photos & Camera, and then select the quality for both video and slo-mo footage.

25> If you turn your iPhone upside down, it won't light up when you get a notification. This won't save masses of power, but over a day it could be enough for that crucial call.

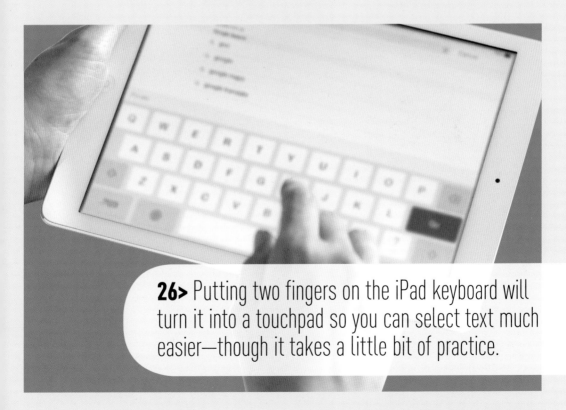

26> Putting two fingers on the iPad keyboard will turn it into a touchpad so you can select text much easier—though it takes a little bit of practice.

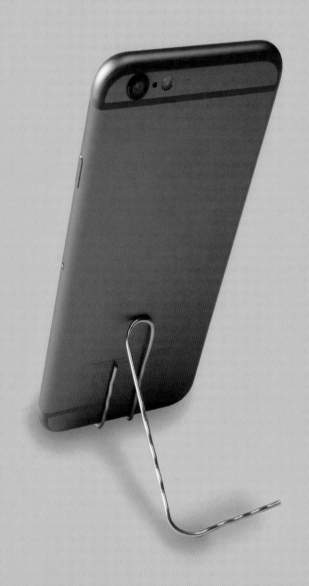

27> Make a DIY phone stand with a large paperclip:

Create your own handy phone stand by following these simple steps:

1. Firstly, straighten out the paperclip so you have a single strip of metal.

2. Bend it in half around a pen so you end up with a large U shape. Lie it down.

3. Twist the two ends of the paperclip upwards, so they're standing perpendicular to the rest of the clip.

4. Now bend the end of the U upwards, so it's also standing up at an angle (this is the back of the stand).

5. Spread the legs of the stand apart, and you now have a little desk stand for your phone.

28> If you haven't discovered Evernote (www.evernote.com), now's the time. It's an app that enables you to save notes, images, and more in the cloud for easy search and retrieval. Better still, it can do the same for web pages.

29> What's your backup regime? If you don't have one, you should. We recommend backing up onto an external hard drive as well as a cloud storage service. Ideally, you want your stuff stored offsite as well as locally.

30> Often lend people things and then forget? Take a picture of them with the item and store it in a special folder in your Dropbox, OneDrive, or on a service like Evernote.

31> If you have a lot of digital photos, consider uploading them to a service like Flickr or Google Photos. Not only will you be able to share them with friends and family, but it's a great way to back them up, too.

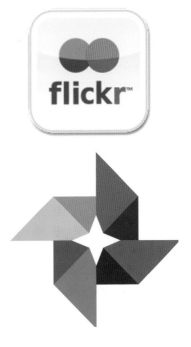

32> If you're in the market for a new printer, look for one with Google Cloud Print—it'll enable you to print from any device, anywhere. Many of these printers are also compatible with AirPrint, which enables you to print from any OS X or iOS device connected to the same network.

20 top hacks for **Android**

33> Find your lost Android by going to www.android.com/devicemanager. Select the device in question and you'll be shown its last available location. You'll need to have location services turned on, but it is on most devices by default, unless you've disabled it.

34> If you like talking to your phone to do web searches, send texts, or set alarms, there's an easier way to do it. Tap the Google search bar on your home screen (or go to the Google app). In the app's settings, go to Voice, then tap OK, Google detection. Turn this on and your phone will listen for you to say, "OK, Google" followed by what you want to search for.

35> Prevent people accessing stuff they shouldn't:

1. Go to Settings > Users.

2. Choose Add User or Profile.

3. Choose Restricted Profile from the pop-up that appears. You'll be asked to enable lock screen security if it isn't already.

4. Choose the apps and content you want that user to have access to.

36> You can now choose to minimize interruption and only get calls from those in your starred contacts list (you can add family and close friends to this list in your Contacts app—just tap the star next to their name). Configure this in Settings > Sound and Notification > Interruptions.

37> Customize Android completely with a launcher app that changes how your home screen operates and looks. The best of these is Nova Launcher.

38> On devices running the standard version of Android, you can access your Notifications with one swipe down from the top of the screen and your Quick Settings (that control Wi-Fi, Bluetooth, Location, NFC, and so on) with a two-finger swipe down.

39> Make your phone super-secure by encrypting all its data. It uses more battery and will take a little while to process initially, but it means that even if somebody plugged your phone into a computer they wouldn't be able to access the data. Go to Settings > Security.

40> Wouldn't it be great to automatically unlock your phone if you were at home? Smart Unlock does just that. Go to Settings > Security > Smart Lock > Trusted Places.

41> You can block calls from a particular contact (and send them straight to voicemail) by going to Edit Contact and tapping the three dots in the top right to bring up the Settings menu. Select All Calls to Voicemail.

42> Use the Recent Apps icon to switch between apps; it looks like one square or two overlapping squares, depending on which Android phone you have. It's usually at the bottom right of the screen. On Samsung devices it's on the bottom left.

43> Whatever Android phone you have, you need to treat it just like a computer—so make sure you remove old apps and widgets. An app can help with this, and there are plenty of options in the Tools section of the Google Play Store, like Power Clean.

44> To remove icons you don't want from your home screen, tap and hold the icon. A remove option (sometimes it's just a garbage can icon) will appear at the top of the screen.

45> Put your contact information on the lock screen in case you lose your phone. Go to Settings > Security. Here you're able to keep information such as your home phone number or email address. If you have a case, why not also attach your contact details to the case in some way?

46> You can add a contact to your home screen so you can directly dial them with a single tap. Press and hold on the home screen, then tap Widgets. Go to Contacts and select Direct Dial.

47> Want to know the name of a song that's playing? Tap the microphone in the Google search bar and ask, "What's this song?".

48> You can change the default apps your phone uses (say, for browsing web pages) in Settings > Apps or Manage Apps. Tap an app name, then tap Clear Defaults. Next time you open a file or page that the default app would have opened, you'll be offered more options as well as the ability to select Always or Just Once.

49> Pushbullet (www.pushbullet.com) enables you to get cell phone notifications to your desktop PC or Mac and reply to them. So you can answer texts, reply to WhatsApp messages, or see when someone mentions you on Facebook without needing to pick up your phone.

50> Use widgets to get instant information. Android phones let you have several home screens onto which you can put widgets as well as apps. Widgets enable you to see at-a-glance details, such as what's in your calendar today. Why not dedicate one of the side home screens to a Gmail widget and a calendar widget for an at-a-glance view of your inbox and appointments?

51> If you need to save your battery, go to Settings > Battery to check out which apps are using the most juice (and quit those you don't need). Different Android phones have different battery-saving apps and technologies built in. Also, turn off technologies that use power, such as NFC and Bluetooth.

52> If your phone has a replaceable battery, it's smart to carry a spare in your bag. Smartphones are pretty power-hungry beasts, and who hasn't been caught short trying to find a place to charge their phone?

53> Don't go out and buy expensive cables—budget ones work just as well.

54> Forgot your plug or adapter in a hotel? You can usually charge from the USB port on the back of the flat-screen TV in your room.

55> Label plugs behind your TV or music system with sticky labels or colored tape.

56> Toilet rolls are great for holding cables together—simply put them vertically in a box for easy storage.

57> The spring from an old pen is a great way to stop charger cables from fraying or breaking—just find the end of the spring and start to twist it around the part of the cable you want to protect. After a little work, the whole spring will be around the cable, preventing any splits.

59> Need to print something, but don't have a printer to hand? Print it as a PDF and save it to your phone, PC, or cloud storage for later printing. This also means you can save any document you want as a PDF!

60> In a browser, holding down right-click and the "S" key on any image on the web has some rather good effects. In Chrome, Google will search for that image in a new tab, so you can find similar images, or a larger version. In Firefox, it makes that image the desktop background (Safari highlights the Use Image as Desktop Picture option). In Internet Explorer, it opens the save dialog box to save the image to your hard drive.

58> Sunglasses are a great way to prop up your cell phone so you can watch a video.

61> Shop around when buying technology or a new phone. You can pick up some great deals. And say no to extended warranties.

62> Bedtime is one of the best times to connect with your partner. It's not one of the best times for checking Facebook.

63> Don't use open public Wi-Fi hotspots, but if you do, make sure sharing is turned off. In OS X, go to System Preferences > Sharing. In Windows, go to Advanced Sharing Settings.

64> Tackle hard-to-open plastic packaging (such as packets containing electric cables) with a can opener to make sure you don't cut yourself.

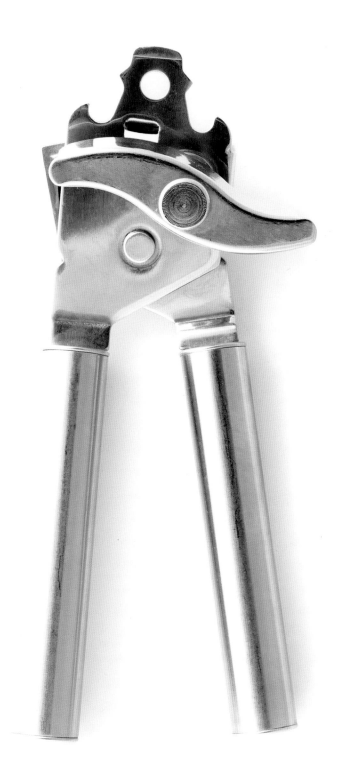

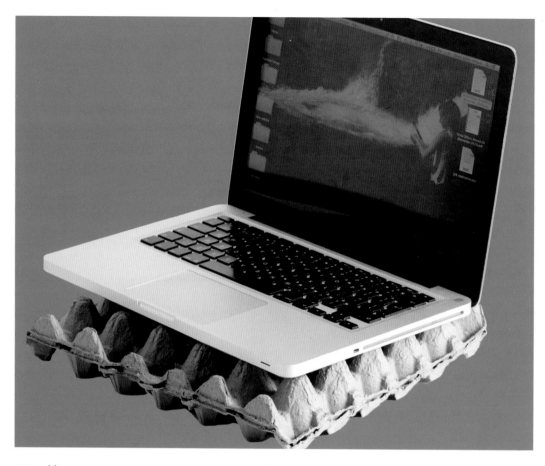

65> You can use an egg tray as a laptop stand, as it cools down your computer (because of the increased airflow underneath the laptop). This is probably most useful for slightly aging or gaming machines.

66> Keep files organized within your Documents folder and your desktop free of clutter. The Downloads folder is where you should keep the bits and pieces you download or get sent as attachments.

67> If you use Spotify, the Spotify Connect feature enables you to use another device as a remote. So you could be playing music through your PC and controlling it with your phone.

68> Keep your keyboard as flat as possible, especially if you touch type. It so happens that those little feet aren't great ergonomically.

69> Use a binder clip to hold cables, such as your phone-charging cable, on your desk.

WORKPLACE HACKS

It is important that the place where you work is comfortable, tidy, and clear of distractions. This will enable you to perform your job at your optimum level. Have a look at these hacks and see what you can introduce to your workplace to help you.

71>
Double use sticky not

Before you thro
a sticky note, u
collect the crum
your keybo

70>
Use binder clips for keyboard feet

If you really like the feet on your keyboard, binder clips can be used if yours are broken.

72> They say tidy desk, tidy mind

And it's true. A cluttered desk doesn't say the right thing to your co-workers and it'll play on your mind, too. You don't have to keep it spotless, but it's best to deal with things when they come in.

73> Keep hydrated

Don't drink enough water at your desk? Have a large clear bottle and mark levels on it with different times of the day (or have a morning and afternoon bottle). You'll soon get the hang of it.

74> Don't be tempted by junk food

Keep a bunch of good-for-you snacks (like granola bars) in your desk drawer or locker if you often need something to nibble on.

20 super tips to power up your **Mac**

75> In Safari, you can see what tabs are open on your other devices. Go to View > Show All Tabs. Google Chrome can also do this on all the devices connected to your Google account.

76> You can share your iTunes Library with other computers on your home network. In iTunes, go to Preferences > Sharing and select Share My Library on my Local Network. You can even select specific playlists.

77> You can send and receive iMessages and text messages on your Mac. You will need to turn on Text Message Forwarding in Settings > Messages on Your iPhone. This works in iOS 8.1, and OS X Yosemite and later.

78> Spotlight search is a great way to launch apps—just search for the app and hit return. You can also do unit and currency conversions here, too!

79> iCloud Keychain is handy for storing your payment information for online shopping, as well as usernames and passwords for sites. It can also store Wi-Fi information so you won't need to re-enter it on another Apple device.

80> Should you wish, you can revert to earlier versions of files. Just hover over the document name when it's open. A menu will appear next to the name. Select Browse All Versions from this menu.

81> You can store whatever files you like on your cloud drive. However, this comes out of your free 5GB cloud allowance.

82> Screen sharing is becoming really common, especially for troubleshooting—you can now do this in OS X; enable it in System Preferences > Sharing.

83> Macs without a DVD drive can share a DVD drive from other (older) Macs. Go to System Preferences > Sharing. Both must be on the same network.

84> You can now make an app completely full-screen using the green Maximize button on the top left of a window.

85> Boot Camp Assistant—in your Utilities folder—lets you run Windows on your Mac.

86> You can now sign PDFs directly from the Mail app. Drag it into your email and hover over it. You'll see a button you can click to view the PDF and perform several functions, one of which is to add your signature.

87> Drop files onto the dock to open an app. Try it!

88> Switch audio outputs and inputs by clicking the volume control as you hold down the Option key.

89> You can opt to start specific apps automatically when you log in. In System Preferences > Users & Groups, go to Login Items.

90> Anybody can temporarily use your Mac with a guest user account. Add one in System Preferences > Users & Groups. Anyone can use this, but any stored information will wipe itself when the user logs out.

91> You can add a keyboard shortcut for whatever you choose in System Preferences > Keyboard > Application Shortcuts.

92> Batch rename files by selecting a bunch of them, right-clicking, and selecting Rename. You can then alter the filenames or add a suffix or prefix.

93> In the latest version of OS X, you can hide the menu bar unless you move your mouse towards it. Open System Preferences, go to General, then click Automatically Hide and Show the Menu Bar.

94> AirDrop enables you to rapidly send files from a Mac to an iPhone, or from an iPhone to an iPad.

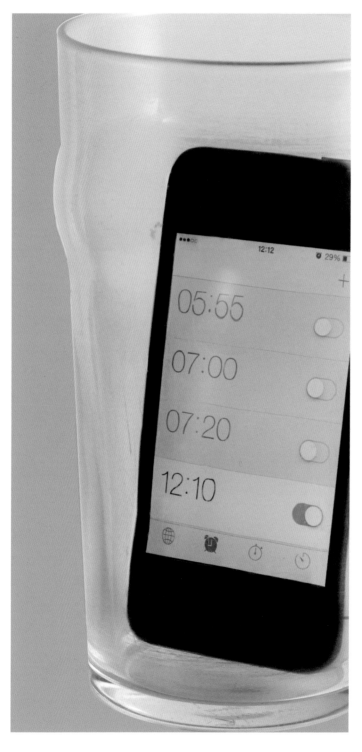

95> An accented letter makes for a strong password, as nobody will guess it.

96> Don't use a laptop keyboard all day long. You should have a proper desktop keyboard, mouse, and monitor when you're at a desk.

97> Marking yourself out as a helpful colleague may sometimes mean people lean on you, but it will also mean that people are happy to perform big favors in return.

98> Don't hear your phone alarm? Amplify it by placing it in an empty glass. You'll soon be awake! You can use just about any container to amplify the sound from your smartphone.

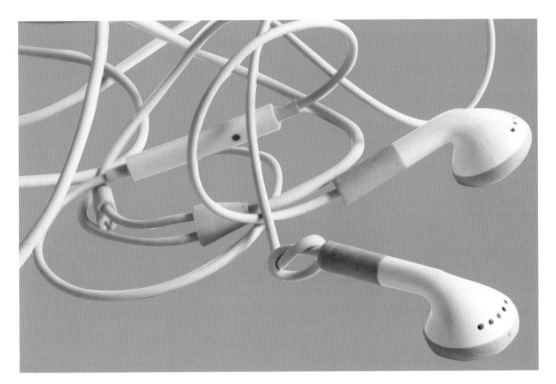

99> Make a little knot in one earphone just below the earbud—you'll always know which is left and which is right.

100> Hair clips are awesome for keeping cables together if no other clip is available.

101> Carry around the earphones that came with your phone—you never know when you'll need to make or take a call hands-free. Don't be one of those people who holds their phone in front of them on speakerphone.

20 ways to get more from **Windows**

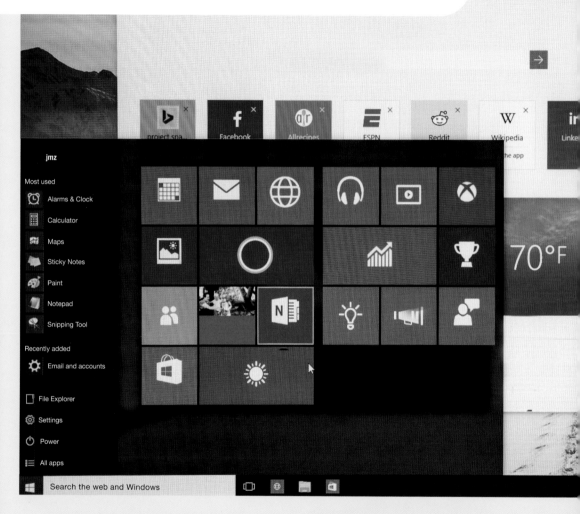

102> To show the desktop at any time, move your mouse to the far bottom right-hand corner—yes, even further than the clock!—and click. All the windows will be instantly minimized and you'll see what's on your desktop. Clicking again will bring your windows back.

103> Most browsers now have a reading view—a way to explore longer-form articles without the distraction of online ads.

104> You might know you can snap windows to the sides of your screen in Windows 7, 8, and 10, but did you know you can use the Windows key plus the arrow keys as a keyboard shortcut for this? If you want it on the right-hand side, press Windows+right.

105> Quiet Hours in Windows 8.1 and Windows 10 enables you to tell the PC that you're busy and stop app notifications and other pop-ups from appearing.

106> Add any folder to the taskbar. Right-click it, go to Send To, and select Desktop (create shortcut). Then, on the desktop, right-click the folder and go to Properties in the menu that appears. Click the Shortcut tab, then, in the target box, add the word "explorer" in font of the text. Now click OK, right-click the shortcut on the desktop again, and choose Pin to Taskbar.

107> You can now scroll down through windows even if you hover over them (the window doesn't have to be active). Enable it in Settings > Devices > Mouse and Touchpad.

108> In Windows 10, you can adjust the size of the Start menu by dragging the sides of the menu. You're also able to add any file, folder, or app by right-clicking it and selecting Pin to Start from the menu that appears.

109> Also in Windows 10, you can right-click the app tiles to bring up icons that enable you to change the size or bin the tile completely.

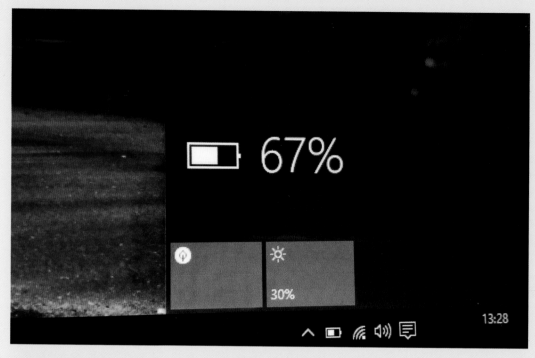

110> Running out of laptop battery? Windows 10 features a new Battery Saver mode that cuts down on everything but the essentials to get those extra minutes you need. Right-click on the battery icon on the bottom right and select Battery Saver.

111> The Send To menu is really useful for copying files to USB drives or a shortcut to your desktop (right-click on any file or folder icon, and select Send To). But if you hold down Shift at the same time as you click, you get even more options in this menu. Very useful.

112> Drag and drop files to and from cloud storage in Windows 10 by setting up OneDrive—it will be available in the notifications area when you first log in. You get 15GB of storage for free.

113> Connect to Bluetooth speakers easily in Windows 10 using the new Connect option in the Notifications Center—click the icon next to the clock.

114> Regularly use particular folders in Windows 10? Pin them to File Explorer's Quick Access panel. Right-clicking on any folder will give you the Pin to Quick Access option. Windows 10 will automatically pin your most-used folders there, too.

115> Open a new window for any of the apps on the taskbar by hitting Windows+1 or another number that corresponds with the icon's position on the taskbar. This is useful if, for example, you knew that Word is Windows+4.

116> Did you like it when apps on the taskbar had labels? Get that back. Right-click on the taskbar to open Taskbar, and Start Menu Properties.

117> If you have a lot of apps open on your taskbar, you can view what's open by pressing Windows+T. Then, just scroll through the apps using the arrow keys.

118> You can also switch between open apps with Alt+Tab, and in Windows 10 there's also a Task View feature—click the icon on the taskbar that looks like a window with another behind it (it's next to the search bar).

119> Get a thicker cursor that's easier to see. In Windows 7, go to the Ease of Access Center in Control Panel, and look for Set the Thickness of the Blinking Cursor. In Windows 8 and Windows 10, go to Settings > Ease of Access > Mouse. On OS X, the option is within Universal Access in System Preferences.

120> You're able to change the options in the Send To menu by going to any File Explorer window and typing just "shell:sendto."

121> If you regularly use Ctrl+C and Ctrl+V for copy in text, remember you can use it for files as well! It's really handy when moving things between folders. Also, when you're in File Explorer, you can open a new window by pressing Ctrl+N and copying from one to another.

122> Email can be the bane of our lives. So, whatever you do, create filters to file or delete emails you don't need to see. If you still have to manually deal with every email you receive, you are wasting time.

123> If people often send you emails but sit nearby, get into the habit of replying to their emails by talking to them as soon as you've received the mail. They'll soon learn to speak to you rather than email.

124> Set up a group chat using something like HipChat (www.hipchat.com).

125> Replying to short emails on your phone is one thing, but if you need to type out a longer email, consider whether it's worth it. Would it be more time-efficient to wait until you have a keyboard to hand?

126> If you need to have a quick conversation with someone and can't do it in person or over the phone, instant messaging using Google Hangouts or Skype can help nip back-and-forth emails in the bud.

127> Consider collaborative document sharing with Google Docs or Office 365, rather than emailing documents back and forth. If you have several versions of the same document in your emails, you're doing it wrong.

128> Gmail's labels can be a great way of referring back to earlier projects. And, because you can have as many labels as you like, you can get quite granular with the categorization.

129> Have a mental separation for emails you're cc'd on. If you're cc'd, it means exactly that—a carbon copy—so do you really need to act on it? You may want to filter emails you're cc'd onto to a separate folder that you can glance at once a day. You could also label them in your inbox.

130> Try and deal with emails as you read them. It's hard to do, but it is possible. If an email needs action on another day, then add it to your to-do list.

131> If someone emails you asking you to forward something, ask yourself why they're asking you to do the dirty work. Are they hiding something? What do they stand to gain? As a general rule, you should feel free to bat this kind of request back.

132> Getting to Inbox Zero is admirable, but it's unrealistic for most of us. Instead, make sure that everything in your inbox still needs to be acted on. Archive or delete the rest.

133> Take time to unsubscribe from email newsletters you no longer want. If you think you might need them at some point, create a filter to skip the inbox and archive them.

134> Don't double up: if you move an email to your task list (perhaps in Outlook or Gmail), then archive the email.

135> Whatever email system you use, make sure you create some Rules (Outlook) or Filters (Gmail). These filter certain types of unimportant emails out of your inbox, leaving space for what matters.

136> Check your task list before you look at your inbox. That way you'll focus on what you really need to achieve.

137> Don't delete useful emails you've finished with (unless they really are trash, in which case delete). Instead, archive them so you can retrieve them later.

14 ways to be more **comfortable** in an office

138> Your monitor shouldn't be closer than 20 inches or the length of your arm. If it's nearer than that, move it.

139> If you can't take regular breaks, look at an object in the distance—like the other side of the office—to reduce eyestrain.

140> If you arrive in a new office, take time to adjust your chair to suit you. You need your back against the back of the chair, and there should be a couple of inches between the edge of the chair and your knees.

141> When buying an office chair, make sure it has good lumbar support. Poor support here will lead to slouching.

142> More and more of us are using standing desks. If you have back problems from sitting all day, ask your employer if they would consider giving you a standing desk.

143> Your chair should be pushed in against your desk, otherwise you'll slump.

144> The top of your monitor should be at eye level.

145> Make sure your forearm is at right angles to your upper arm when you're sitting at the desk. You shouldn't be holding the weight of your arms all the time.

146> Although it's hard, try not to lean or reach forward. Train yourself to keep your back straight and adjust your chair so this is easier to do.

147> Get out of the habit of holding a phone between your head and neck. If you need to be on your phone and use a computer at the same time, use a headset.

148> You should be able to put your entire forearm on your desk when using your mouse.

149> The top of your keyboard should be level with your elbows when typing.

150> Avoid wearing high-heeled shoes if you need to stand for long periods of time.

151> You should not have to move your mouse off the desk surface when in use. If you're doing this, adjust your mouse travel in Windows or OS X.

152> Take time to disengage from work before you get home. Don't spend your commute answering work emails. Do something for you. You need to switch off.

153> If you drive home, listening to entertaining radio can help you switch off from your day in the office.

154> If you are constantly tempted by emails on your phone when at home, temporarily disable your work account during the evening (stop emails synchronizing in your mail app, for example). And definitely don't check them at weekends!

155> If you're in the habit of getting home and ranting to your partner, come up with a time limit for doing this—or make sure you give them equal time to make their feelings heard.

156> If you have a work phone, switch it off when at home, if you're able to do that. Or keep it somewhere during the evening where you won't be tempted to get at it.

157> A more positive way to reflect on the day can be for you and your partner to both say three things that have gone well. So, even if you've had a bad day at the office, you can still focus on the positives in your life.

158> Make sure you're taking the breaks you're entitled to. If you really can't, a walk around the block will help you regroup and refocus.

159> If you often forget to leave the office at lunch, why not set the alarm on your phone?

160> You could set your phone alarm to be the same as your ringtone or a short beep like a text, so it's not obvious to your co-workers what you're doing.

10 ways to make your social profiles **employer friendly**

161> Go incognito in your web browser (so you're not signed in) and Google yourself. Can you see anything you wouldn't want an employer to see?

162> If you're a professional and don't have a LinkedIn profile, you should. It ranks well in Google for your name (providing you're not John Smith) and is a good way of making yourself a legitimate professional.

163> Your Twitter biography is a great place to sell yourself; likewise is the headline of your LinkedIn profile.

164> Your profile picture needs to mark you out as a decent person, but it doesn't need to be a plain portrait.

165> Become a master of Facebook's privacy settings and only mark updates as Public if you really do want them to be public.

170> Remember that things from the past can come back to haunt you, so take time to ensure embarrassing old YouTube videos are removed or privacy is restricted.

166> Remember that anybody can see your Twitter updates. You know that curse-filled tweet you posted about your football team? Might be time to delete it.

167> If there's any chance of your boss taking a dim view of anything you get up to during your time off, then add them to your restricted list.

168> Ask former colleagues for LinkedIn recommendations. They'll almost always be happy to give them (and you can offer to return the favor).

169> You can put Facebook contacts into lists, so you can add work people to a particular list and prevent them seeing certain updates.

The best ways to deal with **conflict** at work

171> Make sure you communicate with others effectively. So much conflict comes from poor communication.

172> Don't bury your head in the sand.

173> If someone is being aggressive towards you, either on the phone or in person, don't be afraid to say something along the lines of, "I will come back later" before leaving. Chances are they will calm down and realize the error of their ways.

174> Learn to deal with conflict. After all, you'll have different views to your colleagues, just as sometimes you have different views to your partner. If you're the boss, you need to stamp it out.

175> Compromise is as important in work as it is in life generally. You won't get everything your own way and it's best to know that from the start.

176> If a situation is troublesome, think of how much it will matter in five years' time. That should give you the perspective you need.

177> If you feel somebody is being particularly nasty, ask them why. Chances are they won't have realized there was a problem or they will defend themselves, in which case you should be prepared to diffuse the situation.

178> If there is one particularly troublesome employee, involve colleagues in the conversation. But be careful your manager doesn't think you're ganging up.

179> Situation completely irretrievable? Consider moving department or quitting your job and looking for another one.

180> Try everything to resolve a problem yourself before escalating it to a boss. Know that you could make your colleague resent you for doing so.

181> You can often diffuse situations by using "I" instead of "you" in difficult conversations. Don't accuse.

182> When others are wading in to an argument, consider why they are doing it. Is there something you could say to them to nip things in the bud?

183> If somebody has upset you, consider what else is going on with them. Do they have issues at home or are they under too much pressure at work? It's worth remembering that sometimes people have baggage they can't leave at the office door.

184> Dealing with conflict quickly will reduce the severity of the problem. Explain where you're coming from and quick.

185> Always accept responsibility for mistakes. Colleagues will appreciate your honesty.

186> Even if you disagree with a management decision, don't go off and do something else on your own. You'll regret it and it could cause problems for yourself.

187> Weigh up each decision you want to rail against. If you don't sweat the small stuff, your manager will be more inclined to listen when you think there is a more serious problem. Keep your powder dry, in other words.

188> Don't just wade in because you feel you need to be involved in a conversation. If you don't have something worthwhile to add, stay out of it.

189> Continually evaluate whether you could have handled a situation better and learn for next time.

190> Gossip is extremely destructive in the workplace. Don't be the office gossip; you never know when you'll need people to depend on.

191> If you don't have a defined job description, it's time you asked for one. You need to know.

192> Be clear on your personal objectives, and those of your team and business. If you're a manager, make sure the people below you know what they should be striving for.

193> Always try to objectively evaluate if you are actually the one with the issue. It's hard.

194> You need to sense check your actions. Often, the best way to do that is to check with a friend. Trusted colleagues are OK, as long as they're not involved.

195> Keep in mind the work style of others and adapt when communicating with them. For example, are they an ideas person, a pessimist, or a laggard?

196> Understand the pessimist's point of view, but show them the positives of the situation.

197> If you have too much work, be honest about it; don't appear as if nothing is wrong. The worst thing is to make promises you then can't keep. This will lead to you letting someone down.

14 top **résumé** and **job-hunting** tips

198> When looking to switch jobs, Google the name of your company and look at all the companies in the "People also search for" section. These are the top targets for your search.

199> Get ready to explain gaps in employment (or gaps in your experience) during an interview. There might be a good reason for them, but these are things you will be required to account for.

200> Consider what's important to put on your résumé at different times. If you edited your college magazine, that may be important immediately after college, but it's insignificant compared to the experience you'll have in five years' time.

201> It's stunning how many people can't write a résumé. Find a decent résumé template on the internet (there are loads for Microsoft Word) and produce something professional. Get ideas from other résumés online.

202> Don't use weird fonts on your résumé. You may think it will set you out from the crowd. Well, it will, but not in a good way.

203> Make sure your cell phone has voicemail set up. You don't want to miss a message during this time.

204> Although it's easier said than done, always have an up-to-date résumé stored on your computer.

205> Make sure you have an email address that isn't silly and just involves your name and maybe a number.

206> If you're in a specialist industry with a lot of competition, it may help to get the advice of a careers professional to refine your résumé.

207> Don't just get updates from the big employment websites, go niche and local. Are there specialist agencies within your field?

208> Make sure your cover letter and résumé are adapted for the job and company you're applying for. Too many potential employees miss out because they haven't bothered.

209> If there are particular employers you're interested in, monitor their Facebook and Twitter feeds. They will probably post jobs there before they go out to job sites.

210> Get somebody else to read your résumé and spell check it (also spell check it yourself, obviously).

211> You don't need to put your date of birth on your résumé, but be aware people will want to know how old you are. It's just a fact of life.

212> Focus on what matters. Keep short-term, medium-term, and long-term goals in mind. The long-term goals don't have to be closely defined, but it does help to know where you're heading and what you'd love to achieve. You can also incorporate wider life choices within this.

213> Equally, know what you would do if you had to leave your job today. Where could you work?

214> If you use freelance help on a regular basis, have a backup plan. Then, when someone leaves you in the lurch, you'll know who to call on as a replacement.

215> Having backup ideas for when things go wrong will mark you out as a good leader or worker worth keeping. You don't need a fully formed contingency plan, but it means you'll remain calm when others start to panic.

216> If your business relies on knowing who people are, get a contact manager like FullContact. You definitely won't regret it.

217> If you need to sign documents on your computer, DocuSign is the best way to do it. It's free for 30 days, and you can even do it from an iPhone.

218> Don't think your workplace will stay the same. Have in your mind that things always change. Even if you have a settled team, know it won't stay that way forever.

219> If you're a leader, consider who else in your business could be valuable to you in a stopgap situation.

220> Always take a photo of business cards people give you.

221> When you're at a professional event, asking for a business card is a good way of drawing a conversation to a close.

222> Unless your job entails being on call or on duty out of hours, make your boss aware if demands are unreasonable, and definitely don't start replying to emails you don't have to.

223> When meeting new people or networking at an event, keep your right hand free at all times so you can shake hands at a moment's notice.

224> If there's an invitee list available to you, make a shortlist of people you absolutely need to meet. Check out their social profiles to see what they look like.

225> If you meet a business contact at an event or social occasion, or were introduced by a friend, take time to follow up. People will remember you made the effort.

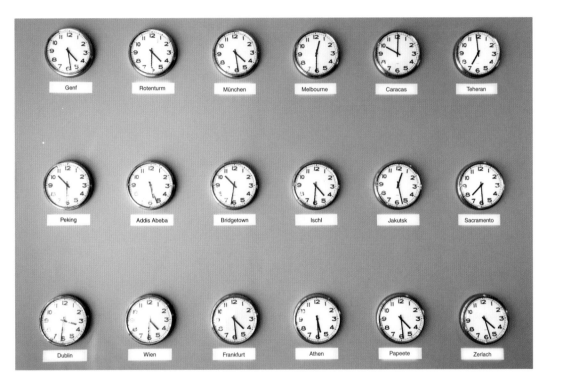

226> Different time zones can be a problem, especially if you work for an overseas company that is clocking off as you clock on. If you're in the habit of replying to their emails before work, as they come in, restrict the time you spend doing this and stick to it. Can you time shift slightly?

2

HOME AND CLEANING

227> A great way to have a good-looking shopping list is to use a picture frame. Get an attractive frame, put some wrapping paper in it (or something else with a neutral background), and then just use a dry-wipe marker to write your lists on it.

228> If you'd rather not have your shopping list on display in the kitchen, paint the inside of a cupboard door with chalkboard paint. You'll then have a hidden family planner.

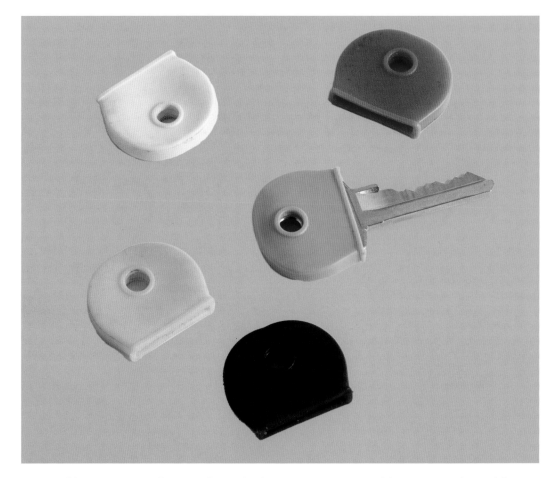

229> If you struggle to identify keys, get yourself some colored key fobs. Or paint the top of the keys with different-colored nail polish.

3 ways you can use lemons to clean

230> Lemons are great for removing stains from metallic bathroom fittings—just rub on the juice and let it do its magic.

231> Large-grain salt and lemons are brilliant for cleaning cutting boards. Sprinkle on the salt, then rub with the half lemons.

232> Clean your microwave easily. Halve two lemons. Put them in a glass dish with water and boil up the mixture in the microwave. Leave for a minute. You'll then be able to wipe down the microwave really easily.

233> Line your garbage can with newspaper so any leaky juices are absorbed. Newspaper is also a worthy substitute for the biodegradable bags you use in a waste-food bin.

234> Always put your keys in the same place—have a bowl or a hook near your front door for them. Train yourself to leave your phone and wallet in the same location so you never struggle to leave the house in the morning.

235> Cover up your thermostat with a hinged, box-framed painting. Get some hinges from the hardware store and attach them to the frame before screwing them onto the wall. Paint the hinges the same color as the wall.

236> A garage ceiling is the best place to store tools and seasonal items. Tools can also go on your garage wall—just look at the different types of storage hooks available in your local hardware store.

237> Hanging is the best way to store things that are different shapes. A towel rail is great for hanging storage in the kitchen, for example.

238> Use adhesive hooks to hide cables around the edge of a table or other furniture.

239> Velcro® strips are handy for keeping remote controls at hand, as you can attach them to a table.

240> Use an old CD rack as an organizer for your bathroom or garage—or even a wooden spice rack.

BATHROOM HACKS

Bathrooms see a lot of traffic. These small, multifunctional rooms can quickly become chaotic and uninviting. Use these hacks to impose some order and create a relaxing oasis.

241> Keep your small implements tidy

A magnetic strip in the bathroom or by your vanity table is the best thing for organizing small metal implements like scissors and tweezers. It can even be a design feature.

242> Not just for eating!

Use spaghetti to prevent burning yourself when lighting hard-to-reach candlewicks.

243> A useful alternative for doorknobs

Doorknobs make excellent towel holders, so paint some wooden ones to match your bathroom.

244> Group your hair-styling accessories

A piece of drainpipe makes a great holder for your hairdryer or curling tongs, especially if you can hide it between a piece of furniture and the wall.

245> Spruce up your mouthwash

Ever thought about putting mouthwash in a decanter to make it look better?

246> Cables can be a pain to store. Use an old, small coat hanger to wind a cable around.

247> A tension rod can make a great space-saver in a kitchen cupboard—especially for items like cleaning sprays; just hook them over the rod. Likewise, you can do this for a second shower rail in the bathroom. Simply use some baskets.

248> Is there a gap beside your fridge? Get a slim sliding shelf and add some small wheels to the bottom to create extra storage. Alternatively, it's a great place for trays or cans.

249> A hanging bathroom storage unit can be a great way to store detergent and other items in your laundry room.

250> Tissue boxes are the best for storing plastic bags, as they make great dispensers.

251> If you pack up an electrical item like a PC or TV, take photos of the back to remember what cable goes in where.

252> Drilling a hole at the base of your garbage can will help you get the bags in and out more easily because there won't be an issue with suction as you take the bag out.

253> Use a hanging shoe rack to store cleaning supplies in a cupboard door.

254> Ironing boards are such a pain in the cupboard. Why not hang it up using two parallel coat hooks?

255> Thumbtacks can be brilliant for hanging up things like sandwich bags and garbage bag boxes on the back of a cupboard door.

11 essential **household cleaning** tips

256> Got glitter everywhere after a birthday celebration? Use modeling clay to clean it up.

257> If you've got a lipstick stain, spray it with hairspray and rub with a damp cloth before putting in the wash.

258> A bit of chalk on a greasy stain can help tease out the oil—this can also be used for fingerprints on walls. Cover the stain, then leave for a few minutes before wiping off.

259> You can clean a mattress with alcohol—proper alcohol. Put vodka into a spray bottle, spray lightly across, then allow to air-dry. The alcohol kills bacteria.

260> Rubbing alcohol on a cloth is the best thing for removing nail polish from a carpet.

261> Rubbing alcohol is also effective for cleaning earphones. Put a little on the end of a cotton swab and watch the crud go.

262> Need to remove paint from clothes? Try a razor; you'll get it off with ease.

263> If you have an iron pan, use sea salt and a sponge to clean it.

264> Blow-dry water rings on a wooden surface as soon as you can and then dab on a bit of olive oil.

265> Clean a clogged-up showerhead by putting some vinegar in a bag and covering the showerhead with it overnight.

266> Rings around the edge of your bath can be easily removed with salt and a halved grapefruit.

267> Toilet and kitchen rolls can be used to keep wrapping paper rolled up. They're also really good in a small box to organize pens and art equipment, like brushes and calligraphy pens.

268> Small Christmas tree lights can be a great way to light up a poorly lit cupboard (providing there's a plug nearby).

269> Putting drawers under the stairs makes a lot of sense. You'll probably need to get them made by a bespoke furniture maker, but they are the best way to use the space.

270> Use an egg carton to store standard-size Christmas baubles—try it, you won't go back to wrapping them up or putting them randomly in a box.

271> Do you have old dust-ridden candles? Rub them with old pantyhose to clean them up as good as new.

272> Store saucepan lids on the cupboard door to save space. It will also prevent a repeat of all those times the lids have crashed to the floor.

273> Slim bookcases can be good for maximizing space in a hallway or between doors. Even better are floating bookcases from a homeware store, as they can be flush to the wall.

274> Coincidentally, you can clean the mess off the bottom of your iron by running it over some aluminium foil covered with a bit of salt. Make sure the iron isn't set to steam.

275> It sounds crazy, but you can always store extra sheets or bedding inside a pillowcase.

10 fantastic uses for **baking soda**

276> Baking soda is the best thing for cleaning silverware. If it's jewelry, combine lemon juice and a small amount of baking soda in a dish, then dip the item in for a minute or two before drying. If it needs more cleaning, leave the mixture on for a couple of minutes before drying. You can do this on a larger scale for silver cutlery and similar (three parts water, one part baking soda).

277> Clean clogged drains with a quarter of a cup of baking soda and hot water on a regular (maybe weekly or fortnightly) basis.

278> A little container with baking soda can freshen up the fridge if it's had an unpleasant smell in it—perhaps you left some perishable food in there when you went on vacation.

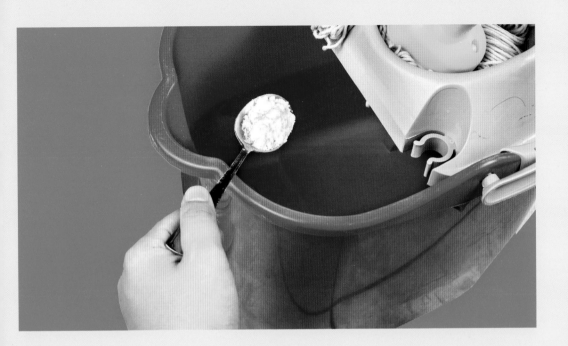

279> Spread a paste of baking soda and water onto vomit. Let it dry, then you'll be able to vacuum the lot up. You can also sprinkle other carpet odors with it and vacuum after 15 minutes.

280> Shower doors and screens can have particularly stubborn watermarks on them. Sprinkle a little baking soda on a wet sponge and wipe. Leave on briefly, rinse, then dry. Use a squeegee if you want a streak-free finish.

281> Spillage on a wooden floor? Baking soda can absorb the liquid that's disappeared into the cracks. Sprinkle it on and vacuum up after a few minutes.

282> If you live in a hard-water area, baking soda can help you stop limescale build-up in your toilet. Pour a couple of cups of baking soda into the toilet, followed by a cup of vinegar. The mixture will foam, but then scrub well with a brush.

283> Treat coffee stains or clean stubborn food residue (on grills or pans) with baking soda. Likewise, it can be good for cleaning garden furniture after the winter, or a wading pool.

284> You can use baking soda as a smell suppressant for used, washable diapers.

285> Combine baking soda with a bit of bleach to clean tile grout. Actually, you can use powder baking soda on its own to clean many sinks and finishes. Don't use it with aluminum, though.

286> Need to find a tiny item like an earring under a cupboard or similar? Use a stocking over the end of your vacuum cleaner, held on with a rubber band.

287> Your dishwasher needn't just be for dishes. Why don't you use it to clean toys or even glass light fittings? You can also wash a sponge instead of throwing it away. Likewise, a hairbrush or even a dustpan and brush.

288> A shelf above a door doesn't alter the look of the room, but is perfect for storing everyday items like toilet rolls, towels, bedding, and more.

289> If you battle with unruly drawers, shoeboxes make really great drawer dividers.

290> Treat wood scratches by rubbing them with a walnut. The oil in the walnut will color up the mark.

291> Use a small brush (like a pastry brush) to get all the crumbs out of your toaster—it makes it so much easier.

292> A lint roller isn't just for cleaning clothes—it's great for getting fluff off stereo speakers and lampshades, too.

293> Spare keys can be a problem. Do you hide them under a stone or flowerpot? Try putting them in a small bottle—like a medicine bottle—then sticking a pinecone or piece of wood to the lid. Bury the bottle in your garden with the pinecone poking out of the ground.

294> When something like a table leg has dented your carpet, use an ice cube. Repeat for really bad dents.

3 unusual uses for **toothpaste**

295> Toothpaste is good for cleaning cloudy car headlights. Just smear it over and buff with a little car wax on a cloth.

296> If your engagement and wedding rings have lost their sparkle, use toothpaste on a cloth to clean them up!

297> If you want to clean and whiten up old sneakers, toothpaste is handy for that, too. Just use it with a bit of water.

298> An old toothbrush is the best thing to clean a keyboard.

299> Moving house? Plastic wrap is a great way to prevent drawers from sliding out of furniture. You can also get industrial wrap for the purpose, which can be used to protect other items.

300> Dismantling furniture? Use food bags in which to store the screws, and tape them to the item in question. Make sure you write on the label in case they get separated.

301> Broken a glass and don't want to pick up the shards? Press a piece of bread onto them—but don't press too hard, of course.

302> Need to dry out really wet shoes overnight? Open them up and stick some newspaper inside.

303> If you have a problem with pet hair on your carpet, try using a squeegee to scrape it off. You can also use a wet rubber glove.

304> Revitalize an old couch—use a spray bottle to squirt on a little rubbing alcohol, then rub it in with a white sponge. Finally, use a brush to fluff it up and it will look a whole lot better.

305> If you have an air-conditioning vent you're fed up with dusting, get a washcloth and douse it with cleaner. Then wrap it around a table knife and use it as a tool to clean the vent.

306> A paper towel covered with a few drops of vegetable oil—that's what you need to clean off a greasy stovetop or backsplash.

307> If you've got a badly scratched leather couch or seat, some appropriately colored shoe polish can buff the gash or discoloration. Be very sparing!

308> You can clean curling tongs with rubbing alcohol— just dab some on with a cloth.

309> Need to tumble-dry clothes in a hurry? Throw in a DRY towel as well to speed things up.

310> You can use some aluminum foil as a tumble-dryer sheet.

311> If you use a dryer sheet in your tumble dryer, don't throw it away afterwards—they make great cloths for screens, baseboards, or desks. The anti-static is great for repelling dust.

312> Dropped your smartphone in liquid? Stick it in rice right away. Yes, it really does work.

Don't just drink **cola**. You can also use it for...

313> Cola can be used to remove stains from some fabrics—including bloodstains. Just rub it on before washing.

314> Cola can also be used to clean the stubborn discoloration of grout between tiles.

315> Got oil stains on the floor of your garage? Use cola to clean them up.

316> Likewise, you can use cola to remove pen and marker stains from a carpet. Pour a little on, rub it in, then clean off with water.

317> If you don't have a scourer to hand when washing up a tray or glass dish, use a screwed-up piece of aluminum foil.

318> Cloudy glassware? You probably don't want to do this for every glass you've got, but spray the best with white vinegar before wiping with a paper towel.

319> Want a less chemical way of cleaning your toilet? Get a jar with a lid, fill it with vinegar, press a small hole into the lid, and place it in the cistern. The vinegar will keep your bowl nice and clean with each flush.

320> If you have a carpet stain you've never been able to get rid of, try this. Get a spray bottle and mix a solution of two-thirds water and one-third vinegar. Spray it on liberally. Then put an iron on a hot steam setting and press it on for 30 seconds. Repeat if you need to.

321> Clean up blinds with a diluted vinegar mixture—use an old sock over your hand and dip it into the solution. Then just run your hand over the blades of the blind.

322> A cutting board placed on an open drawer is a great way to maximize countertop space if you've got a lot to do and not much work surface.

323> If you like to change things around in your garden, bury some large pots and place flowerpots within them—then you can swap around the plants whenever you feel like a change.

324> Need to clean hard-to-reach places like the corners of a high ceiling? Put a towel on the end of a broom and brush away.

325> A muffin tin is an excellent thing to grow plants in if you haven't got much space. It's also handy to space out plants in the garden.

8 super **kitchen** cleaning tips

326> Got a portable grill or sandwich toaster? After cooking, place two damp paper towels into the press and close. This will steam clean the grill. Wipe down after.

327> Clean a dishwasher until it sparkles—run it with nothing inside except an open, dishwasher-safe container of white wine vinegar on the top shelf. Then run it again on a hot quick wash, having sprinkled some baking soda into the bottom.

328> Clean a blender by putting some soap and water into it, and turning it on for a few seconds.

329> Clean stainless-steel appliances with a sponge and a little cream of tartar (otherwise known as potassium bitartrate).

330> Clean a coffee pot by boiling up an equal solution of vinegar and water. Leave it for an hour and repeat. Don't forget to run a couple of cycles of clean water through afterwards, to prevent your coffee from tasting weird.

331> Badly burnt pan? Fill it with water and two cups of vinegar. Boil it up. Take it off the heat and add two tablespoons of baking soda.

332> Got stubborn stains on the sides of your microwave? Remove by putting a dish in the microwave with some water and dishwashing liquid. Turn it on to high power for one minute, then wipe it down with a wet sponge.

333> You can use half a white onion to clean off a grill while it's still hot.

3

DO IT
YOURSELF

334> If you're worried about splitting the bottom of a piece of wood when inserting a nail or screw, use a length of waste wood underneath.

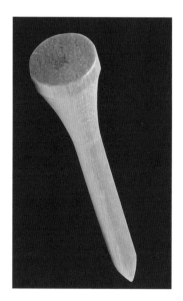

335> Do you have a screw or nail hole that's way too big? Repair it with a piece of doweling or even a wooden golf tee—hammer it in lightly, then cut it off flush with a small saw.

336> Screwing into wood, but it's really tight? Put a little soap on the screw to help it in.

337> Turn a small decorative picture frame into a key holder. This is best with a frame that has a bit of depth to it, so you can screw some small hooks into the inside of the frame to hold your keys.

10 super uses for **coffee grounds**

338> Cats don't like coffee grounds, so if you have some troublesome felines—perhaps going to the bathroom in the wrong place—try grounds as a deterrent.

339> Coffee grounds are useful for cleaning oily hands—they'll absorb the troublesome grease.

340> Used in a paste with vinegar and warm water, grounds can be used to remove scratches from furniture.

341> Sprinkle grounds on top of meat—they work as a tenderizer as they soak up excess moisture.

342> Coffee grounds are fantastic for compost heaps, mostly because worms love them. The best recipe is an equal mixture of grounds, fresh-cut grass, and leaves.

343> You can also use grounds to clean a dirty grill pan. Create a cleaning solution by mixing the grounds with soapy water. The coffee acts as an abrasive, which is why it's ideal for stubborn stains.

344> You can also use coffee as a fine mulch to prevent weed growth.

345> Slugs and snails hate the acidity of coffee grounds— so sprinkle some on paths and in flowerpots.

346> Nitrogen in the coffee means the grounds are a great fertilizer for things such as carrots, tomatoes, green vegetables, and even roses.

347> Grounds can also neutralize pests on pets—
just rub some into their fur after shampooing.
The reason is that fleas don't like coffee.

349> Avoid splitting wood when you hammer in nails. First, find the spot you want to nail into. Then lightly tap the head of the nail against the spot at right angles to the direction of the grain. The indentation will mean the wood doesn't split.

350> If you want to prevent a basic latch door from closing, use a rubber band crossed over between the two handles.

351> Hanging up rollers and brushes will keep them in the best condition, and enable them to dry properly after cleaning.

352> Clean a glue gun while it's still hot, using aluminum foil.

348> A staple remover is a great way to hold a keyring open so you can add or remove keys.

353> Cut a slot in the top of a key to locate it faster in the dark.

354> Put gloves over the top posts of a ladder to prevent marking painted surfaces.

355> If you need to remove a nail and protect the wall or wood behind, use a putty knife.

356> You really can use old newspaper to clean dirty windows instead of a cloth or paper towel.

357> Got a puncture in a bicycle or stroller tire? Remove it, then pump it up and hold it underwater to see where the puncture is.

358> You can keep a hose in place by tying a knot.

359> Stand up a flashlight with a length of thick copper wire—perhaps four inches. Bend the two ends to make legs, then fashion the rest into a bent U-shape that can cradle the flashlight. If you have very thick wire you can even bend it around the flashlight itself, then make a simple stand just by bending four to six inches of wire into a zigzag shape.

360> Use a clothespin to hold a nail in place when hammering. A comb also works.

361> Regulate greenhouse heat by leaving the door open on really hot days. A thermometer is a greenhouse essential.

362> Use old kitchen cupboards as garage storage. Not only can you store stuff within the cupboards themselves, but also on top of them.

363> Have you thought about painting the edge of your door to add a splash of color?

364> Do you have storage units with sections that are too tall? Insert small shelves standing on mason jars or tin cans to elevate the items at the back.

365> Fold over the end of the adhesive tape to keep your place. Also, don't buy cheap tape that's too thin to use properly.

20 painting tips for **brilliant** results

366> A lot of paint colors are pretty accurate nowadays, but if you're unsure you can always mix several cans together in a large bucket.

367> If your paintbrush is overloaded as you paint into a corner or along an edge, begin a couple of inches away from it, then edge the bristles into the corner gradually, so you don't get a big sludge.

368> It's tedious, but it really does pay to sand bumpy or old painted walls (and take time to fill in chips and holes with primer first).

369> If you're painting a wall next to a textured ceiling, run a screwdriver along the edge of the ceiling, so you can run the brush bristles into it and "cut in" the edge.

370> When using a roller, make sure you roll over the edge of the previous stroke to avoid a mark. Roll the full height of the wall. Alternatively, feather out the paint instead to avoid marks.

371> You can press masking tape down on gloss and wood with a putty knife to prevent paint bleeding through.

372> Canvas makes a really good floor protector, as it doesn't let any paint through. Always avoid thin bed sheets because the paint could soak through.

373> Once you've sanded, wipe off the walls. You could use a cloth for this, but a floor mop can work well for larger areas. Make sure you wash the mop out properly.

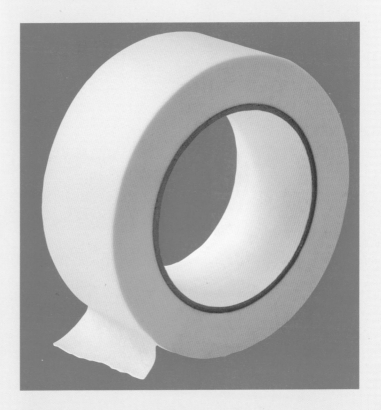

374> Masking tape is essential—especially to protect your baseboards—but be very gentle when pulling it off, so you don't mess up your edges.

375> Always finish one wall before starting another—it's not a good idea to do the edges of all the walls first, as you won't get a consistent finish.

376> If you're painting a carpeted room, buying some adhesive floor covering can help you if you're particularly messy or are worried about making marks (but dropped paint WILL get on the soles of your shoes as it doesn't dry that quickly). Otherwise, drop cloths should be fine. Old curtains make great drop cloths.

377> With gloss, it's worth remembering that the undercoat gives the color and the topcoat the finish. So be sparing with the gloss coat—you're just applying a sheen. This simple advice will help you avoid putting on too much and causing drips (you'll still get some drips—you always do).

378> Give your roller a nice warm water wash before starting painting with water-based paint—the paint will go on a lot easier and not be quite as spray-tastic.

379> If you are painting the kitchen, wipe down with a degreaser first—you need a clean wall to paint.

380> If the thought of clearing up your oil-based paint tray is putting you off painting, then line it with cellophane.

381> If you're painting an old window, don't worry about using masking tape on the glass. Instead, scrape it off the glass afterwards—unless you make a real mess, it's much easier.

382> If you've been using oil-based paint, soak the brush in a jar of turpentine overnight.

383> Don't skimp on paint. When you dip your brush into the pot and it comes out stacked with paint, it's tempting to scrape some off. But you want that paint on the wall, so just get rid of the excess drips and start spreading it on.

384> Invest in some cleaning wipes that can be used on your hands. You'll be able to get paint off much more easily.

385> Old paintbrushes can be revived if you soak them in vinegar (or turpentine, but vinegar is cheaper).

386> Cut off a piece from a large spool of paper or plastic by standing the roll on its end and cutting downwards—it's a lot easier to do. For wrapping paper, you can use a kitchen knife or pocketknife if you make a fold in the paper first. The knife needs to be sharp, though, or you'll tear the paper.

387> Repair a broken zipper pull with a safety pin— a paper clip can work temporarily if you're stuck.

388> If you have an untidy shed or laundry room, why not build or buy some large shelves (they could be plastic) on which you can store big plastic boxes? Ration boxes to family members or for different purposes, and don't allocate more space elsewhere!

389> A C-clamp on the side of a ladder can be really handy for holding tools while you're off the ground.

390> Find the right drill bit for drilling a hole by using an adjustable wrench as a makeshift measurement device.

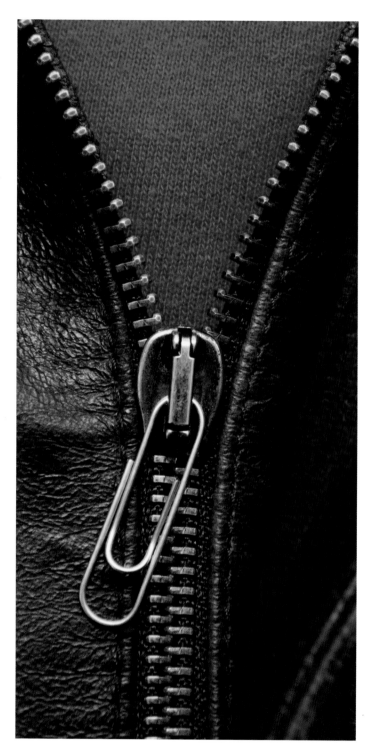

391> Once you've opened a tin of paint, wrap a rubber band lengthways around the entire tin, so it's across the opening at the top. Use it to wipe excess paint from your brush—that way you won't have to wipe your brush on the side of the tin, which builds up gunk.

392> If you have a heavy drawer that often gets stuck, see if you can stick some strips of plastic on the runner to help it in and out more easily. Thin but strong plastic is required, such as that from a plastic detergent bottle.

393> Often pull an old wooden drawer out too far? Make a mark on the drawer so you know how far it'll go.

394> If you need to find the same point on both sides of a wall that separates two rooms—say you want to make sure there are no electric cables where you're going to be drilling—then measure the same distance from the doorframe (or something else, like an opening or hatch) between the two rooms. Ensure you have the right place by also measuring down from the ceiling.

395> Far-sighted and lost your glasses? Pierce a piece of card and peer through the hole for a quick fix.

396> If you need to replace the handle on a spade, fork, or other garden tool, make sure the oval wood grain is on the side of the handle for strength. So, if you were looking at the face of the spade, you wouldn't be looking at the grain.

397> Putting up stud walling? Bear in mind you'll need extra boarding anywhere you plan to install bookshelves or other weighty wall-hanging furniture, like a cabinet.

398> Hang your bicycle on the garage wall using a couple of hooks. You'll save a lot of space.

5 great tips for looking after **grass**

399> Don't cut your grass too short—it will look patchy and brown, especially if it's the height of summer and you're in a drought area. It also may not grow healthily. Go for about a third of the current height of the grass.

400> If you have to cut grass that's a bit damp, go slowly. Cutting it fast won't get the result you want and you may find you're just flattening it, rather than actually cutting it. But, generally, mow when it's dry.

401> You don't have to clean up grass clippings from the lawn. The cut grass (unless it's in clumps) will actually return nutrients to the lawn. Just lightly rake out clumps.

402> Mowing a big area? Look ahead. Looking down means you won't mow in a straight line.

403> When mowing the grass, do the edges first to give yourself room to work with. Don't try to cut the difficult bits (like near a rock garden) and damage your blade. Just accept you'll have to do some by hand.

404> Don't over-tighten the washer in a faucet, as it will lead to leaks. Also, to avoid damage, try not to grip the faucet directly with pliers—use a piece of wood or cardboard in between.

405> Use an old jug, vase, or other old item as a planter to add interest.

406> Need to glue a couple of flat things together? Use a pile of heavy books as a press.

407> Put some caulk on the bottom of rugs to stop them moving around on hardwood floors.

408> Stand barbecue coals in a drink carton to form a protective shield against the wind as you light up—the coated carton will also work wonders to get things going.

409> If you have a stud wall that isn't covered over on the garage side, use it for vertical storage. By nailing some batons across, you can restrain many items; while mini shelves can be used for other items, such as car-care kits or outdoor toys.

410> If you have several recycling boxes, you'll know storing them can take up a lot of space. Fitting some simple wall mounts means you can put them above each other.

WORKSHOP HACKS

It's easy for your workshop or toolshed to become cluttered with equipment. Try some of these hacks to ensure that you can always find what you're looking for without wasting time.

411> Another use for baby food jars

Baby food jars are ideal for keeping small amounts of paint handy. Don't forget to take the original labels off so there's no way they can be confused with something else.

412> Keep nails and screws handy

Put a small magnet on the bottom of tools (like a hammer) to hold nails or screws.

413>
Keep tools handy

If you have a tool you often need in your workshop, stick it somewhere you can easily locate it using Velcro® strips or by embedding it in putty.

414> Need to unscrew a stripped screw?

Use a rubber band in between the screw and your screwdriver.

415> Reuse old food containers

Store nails and pins in mini mason jars or other old food containers with lids. With small mason jars, you could even stick the lids to the underside of a shelf for easy access, and then just unscrew the jar when you need something.

416> Wooden wine boxes make amazing-looking planters.

417> By using rain barrels on various levels, you can get water to different areas of your garden. Use pallets or cinder blocks (or a natural feature like a bank) to raise them up.

418> Old tires are fantastic for creating a rock-garden effect without the rocks. Why not paint the tires, too?

419> Short pieces of polyvinyl chloride (PVC) piping screwed to the wall make excellent storage for garden tools.

420> Bubble wrap makes good greenhouse insulation.

421> Remove stagnant water using a hose. Suck on the end that is lower than the water to draw it up, then drop the hose very quickly!

422> If you have plants that need cooler temperatures during hot periods, put them outside the greenhouse during the day.

423> Got a wooden garden tool that's finished its useful life? Cut the tool end off and shape the handle to a point. You now have a dibble for making holes to plant seeds.

424> Cutting plywood by hand? Apply masking tape before cutting to prevent splintering of the edges as you cut (you will still get some, however).

425> Hang flowerpots on a fence for a more interesting display—use trailing plants for more dramatic effect.

10 DIY **car hacks**
worth knowing

427> You know those sticky mat things for electronic devices that taxi drivers always seem to have? Well, guess what? They have them because they work. You'll never wonder where you put your phone again, and it'll always be mounted where you can get to it.

428> Radiator leaks can be temporarily plugged in several ways. The best thing is to use a car leak repair product. But if you don't have a car store near you, or you're desperate, then break an egg into the radiator. It will cook in the hot water and force itself into the leak.

429> Often get a frosty windshield when parking outside? Check out what direction the sun rises from and note how it spreads over the road where you live. Does the sun hit a patch somewhere else before it hits where you park? You may be better off parking elsewhere and saving yourself the time it takes to defrost the car.

430> If you have trouble judging the distance when parking in your garage, hang a tennis ball from the ceiling in the right position. Park your car in the right place, then work out where the ball needs to hang, and attach it with a hook and some string.

426> Got a small dent in your car? If you're not that worried about the car (in other words, it's not worth getting it done professionally), you may be able to get the dent out yourself using a sink plunger. Yes, really.

431> You can use hand sanitizer as a de-icer because of the alcohol content. This can also be handy for freeing up a lock if you need to get into your garage.

432> A bungee net—usually used for securing stuff to a motorbike—is great for extra storage in cars. Simply stretch it across the "ceiling" of the car between the handles above your doors (obviously you'll need to make sure the bungee is big enough). They don't cost much and provide some really useful storage.

433> If, like us, you've been in the situation where your car's fuel line is ruptured, it can be rather annoying. If you've got chewy candy or gum to hand, you may be able to plug the hole temporarily. You'll need to get it repaired pretty soon, though. Make sure you clean off the area around the leak before sticking.

434> Many of us have messy cars, but a plastic ice-cream container can make a good wastebasket if you cut a hole in the lid. Some people also recommend a plastic cereal dispenser (probably for bigger cars). Line the wastebasket with a plastic bag so you don't have to keep cleaning the container itself.

435> If there's a sticker on the windshield that you just can't get off, get some wet newspaper and slap it over the top. Fifteen minutes later, the water will have soaked into the sticker and you'll be able to remove it.

436> Always use a bungee cord when using a hand truck to hold the goods in place.

437> Use an old glove as a holster for small tools and hardware.

438> Stuck zipper? Use a graphite pencil on the teeth to make it easier to move.

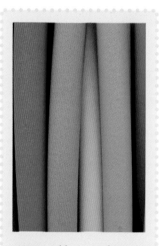

439> Use a foam swimming pool noodle to prevent hitting your car door on the wall of your garage.

440> Water greenhouse plants in the evening. That way, the water won't evaporate in the heat of the day.

441> Gardeners have always put old pottery in the bottom of flowerpots (known as "crocks") to aid drainage—especially if heavy, clay-rich soil is used. But you can just as easily use a pile of old beer bottle caps instead. While you're at it, you could put a bit of gauze over the holes in the bottom of the pot to stop creepy-crawlies getting in.

442> You can make an ace garden potting table out of stacked pallets, and then either paint or creosote it.

443> Use painted chicken wire to create interesting garden shapes or decorations.

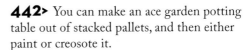

444> Using a nail to punch holes in a detergent bottle creates a good makeshift watering can.

4

FASHION

445> Remember that casual clothing doesn't have to be boring. How about buying some colors to brighten up your wardrobe?

446> If you're shopping for a special outfit for an important occasion, such as a wedding, you're better off going with your hair and makeup resembling how it will be on the day.

447> You don't need to spend lots to have a great closet. There are plenty of discount stores selling brilliant clothes. They sell a lot of terrible clothes, too, of course, so you need to hunt out the decent ones!

448> Have difficulty doing up the back of your dress? Use a piece of string and a safety pin.

449> When you're in a store trying on clothes, why not try something that's completely out of your comfort zone? You'll soon learn what you can get away with (or if it's too much!). Who knows, though, you might like it...

CLOSET HACKS

As we dip into our closets every day to select clothes to wear, it's easy to misplace garments and accessories. Here are some clever closet hacks to help you keep your clothes in order.

451> Hang up your jeans

Shower curtain hooks are brilliant for hanging up jeans.

450> Locate T-shirts easily

Store T-shirts or tops vertically in a drawer so you can see them all without difficulty.

452> Brighten up outfits with accessories

Remember that accessories can give a drab outfit a new lease of life or burst of color. Scarves are especially good.

453> Always losing one glove?

Use a safety pin to keep gloves together or turn them into each other if that doesn't spoil them.

454> Clever storage

Use a paper towel holder to organize your bangles.

455> Makeup spillage in your handbag? Use a damp cloth to pick it all up.

456> Mason jars make great makeup organizers.

457> Letter or magazine organizers are great for keeping flip-flops, hats, or bags organized.

458> Stains can spread if you rub them. Always dab the stain instead, unless it's a grass stain or similar, when the best thing to do is use some toothpaste on it.

459> Magnets are the best (and most decorative) way to arrange bathroom makeup—get a magnetic strip and stick mini-magnets to your makeup items.

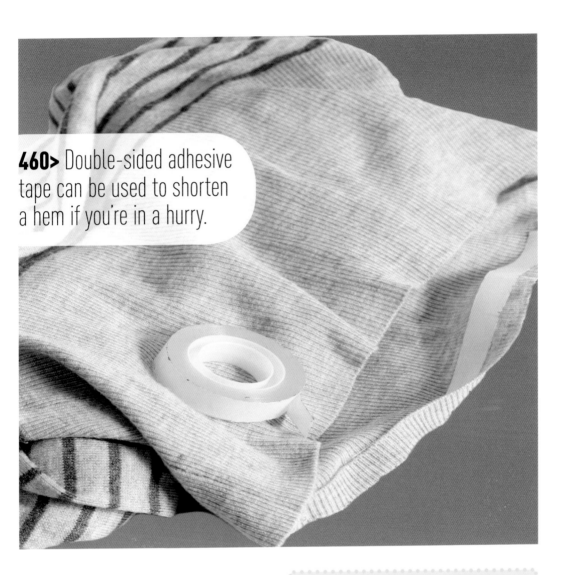

460> Double-sided adhesive tape can be used to shorten a hem if you're in a hurry.

461> Another shortcut to hemming (that will last longer than tape!) is to use a hot glue gun.

462> Got an old but decent coat that's looking tired? A good tailor can help. Why not replace the buttons or even the lining?

463> Get fashion feedback from those you love and trust. They won't flatter you like the sales clerk in a clothing store.

464> Don't go heavy on brand names. Would you buy something if it didn't have branding on it? If the answer is no, then you know what to do.

9 tips for looking after **shoes and boots**

465> After getting work boots or hiking boots dirty, clean them to prolong their life. Brush off with a cloth or a brush if you need to.

466> Don't take shortcuts to breaking in shoes or boots (like soaking in water or heating with a hairdryer). The likelihood is you'll damage the boot and they'll be uncomfortable. Just wear them.

467> Clean up scuff marks on boots by rubbing with a cloth and some hand soap.

468> If you like formal-type shoes for most occasions, try an ankle boot for something different.

469> Don't put leather boots or shoes on or near a radiator to dry. Let them air dry (in front of a fan is OK).

470> If water doesn't bead up and run off the surface of your boot, it's time to re-waterproof. You need to treat them regularly, anyway, to prevent cracking.

471> Don't kick boots off at the heel—doing this repeatedly will damage the boots.

472> Clean white shoes by firstly using a brush or cloth to get rid of excess dirt. Then remove the laces and rinse the shoes under warm water. After, scrub with soapy water and a brush before letting them drip-dry (stuff them with paper towels—but don't use newspaper, as it will run).

473> Could some new colorful laces and a polish transform a tired pair of shoes?

474> If you get a hole in your pantyhose, take them off and apply nail polish around the hole to stop it spreading. Clear polish is best so it doesn't look obvious.

475> Hairspray can also be used to prevent holes in pantyhose, as it is sticky.

476> Going out to a club or to see a band? Make sure what you're wearing is comfortable. You don't want to be in the bathroom every half hour adjusting yourself.

477> A carabiner is superb for holding hair accessories.

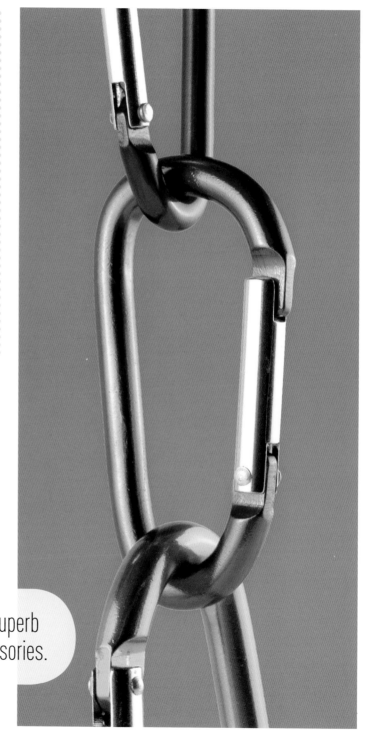

478> For a big occasion, stick to what you know best—clothes you feel comfortable in and/or match your shape. A combination you've tried before is a good idea!

479> When buying jeans, the first thing you should check is whether they're designed to shrink after the first wash. Some jeans are designed to shrink as much as 10 percent.

480> Pumice stones are great for de-bobbling a sweater.

481> You can purposely shrink jeans by washing them on a hot, non-delicate cycle, then drying them on the hottest setting possible. You might need to repeat the process.

482> Got problems with bobbling on a sweater? Use a rough kitchen sponge to remove the bobbles and revitalize your sweater.

483> Packing jeans?

A pair of jeans can be a bulky item of clothing to pack. To make the most of your space when packing clothes, follow these three simple steps to fold your jeans:

1. Fold the pair of jeans in half to begin with so that the legs are on top of each other.

2. Fold them lengthways in half, back over on themselves.

3. Then fold them lengthways in half again.

484> If you don't have time to try on jeans, try the neck method; put the waist of the jeans around your neck. If they're not too tight they should be OK.

485> Although some modern washing machines get good results with lower-temperature washes, the rule has always been that the hotter the wash, the cleaner soiled clothing will be, especially if it's white.

486> Wash cashmere and other wool items by hand. It's just not worth the risk. Mind you, it's worth paying attention to care labels on every sensitive item.

487> A pants hanger makes a great recipe holder in the kitchen.

488> After ironing, let the shirt or dress hang for a few minutes before putting it on. Otherwise you might re-crease it.

489> Beeswax is a great way to put a water-resistant coating on your shoes.

490> Talking of wax, if you get candle wax on clothing, then scrape off the excess (with not too sharp a knife); put paper towels on top and underneath, then iron the top paper towel. The paper towels will absorb the wax.

491> It's best to iron clothes when they're slightly damp.

492> Get rid of oil stains on leather by sprinkling the stain with baby powder or talcum powder, and leaving overnight. You can repeat the process until the stain has disappeared.

493> Even if you use an underwear wash bag, prolong the life of delicate underwear by not washing them with heavy items, such as towels or jeans, as they could cause damage.

494> Got a white deodorant mark? Rub the stain off with a bit of foam or a pair of pantyhose.

495> White wine remains the best way to help remove red wine stains.

11 great uses for **petroleum jelly**

496> False eyelashes you can't remove? Rub some petroleum jelly on with a cotton swab and leave for a minute before removing.

497> You can also use a small amount on real eyelashes to tidy them up.

498> It will soften your cuticles and make your fingertips less rough.

499> It's great for massaging into the cracked skin on your feet before bedtime (put on some clean socks afterwards). Equally, rough elbows can be salved, and it's great for chapped lips too, of course.

500> It can be used to prevent or soothe any chafing or soreness caused by clothing.

501> If you're dyeing your hair, apply it around your ears and across your forehead so you don't stain your skin, too.

502> You can use it to release stuck rings (dishwashing liquid can also be good for this).

503> It can also re-shine nail polish that's been applied for a few days.

504> You can use it as a way to highlight your eyes —don't get it in your eyes, though! You could also mix it with a little eyeshadow to make it shiny. It also shines up leg bronzer.

505> Add some extra shine to shoes by dabbing a little bit of it onto them.

506> Likewise, it will also act as a lubricant to make inserting earrings pain-free. It especially helps if you don't often wear earrings.

507> A well-fitting black leather jacket is a great addition to any male closet.

508> Wear a new leather jacket in the rain to break in the leather and enable it to stretch to your shape.

509> Watermarks can be removed from leather by brushing on a solution of vinegar and cold water until you can no longer see the stain. Then let it dry.

510> Re-waterproof a jacket by using a two-in-one washer and re-proofer (you can do this in a machine or by hand).

511> Attach a safety pin to the bottom of your pants to avoid static build-up if you have problems with particular carpets, say at work.

512> Hair straighteners make great mini-irons to get a straighter shirt collar.

513> The best way to get your feet used to new shoes is by first wearing them around the house for a few evenings.

514> Clip-on earrings or brooches make great embellishments for otherwise dull, flat shoes.

515> If you buy vintage clothes, chances are they'll smell a bit. Put one part vodka and two parts water in a spray bottle to freshen things up.

516> Don't wear brand new shoes when you know you're going to be on your feet for hours.

517> You can stretch shoes that are too tight in the freezer. Fill a freezer bag with water and place it in each shoe. Freeze overnight.

518> Diamonds can be kept sparkling with a bit of dishwashing liquid on an old toothbrush.

519> Forget about regularly washing swimwear in the washing machine. The elasticity will gradually go. If you want to wash it at the end of a holiday, use an underwear/delicates wash bag.

520> Don't put bras in the dryer. If you hang them to dry naturally, do so between the cups rather than by the straps to prevent any misshaping.

521> Only button up the top button of any suit or blazer.

522> Often get creased clothing as it's been at the end of the closet? Use a rubber band wrapped around the rail to stop the final garment being pressed against the wall.

523> For women, you don't want to show too much skin in a professional environment. A good rule of thumb is to only show one body area—so if you're wearing a short skirt, cover up on top.

524> Why not arrange your clothes in color order from dark to light? You won't lose a shirt again.

525> When washing, we all end up with single socks. Store all of your single socks in one place—say, in a plastic bag in your drawer—then match them up every few months.

526> For weddings, a white shirt is best. For other occasions, there's nothing wrong with a classic single-color shirt.

527> Many shirts come with plastic collar stays, but you can invest in metal ones if you want to keep your shirt pristine. While sterling silver ones are available, you can spend considerably less.

528> As you tend not to have too many belts, opt for good-quality leather, so they look smarter and last longer.

529> Remember, you can get extra holes punched in a belt should you need it. Your local shoe repairer should be able to help you.

530> A silk handkerchief is a classic look. Use it when you don't want to wear a suit and tie, but need to add some class to a jacket.

531> Match your belt with your shoes for an extra bit of class. Belts shouldn't be too showy. Simple is best.

532> A dimple in your tie can make it seem a little less formal. You'll need a decent quality tie to do this.

533> Even if your company has a dress-down policy, what's wrong with making an effort? Remember, you never know what kind of day you will have.

534> Tie clasps (or tie clips) look good in formal situations and communicate to others that you care about your appearance. But they also have a practical use—to hold the two ends of your tie together. The bar shouldn't go across the full width of the tie.

535> Spare clothing is handy, especially if you are often in formal situations. So keep a spare shirt or blouse at the office, or perhaps a whole change of clothes in the back of the car. This is essential if you have kids or animals, or your job requires you to visit clients.

5 ways to care for **suede**

536> Use a stale bread crust to clean suede.

537> Scuffs can be removed with an eraser.

538> For more serious dirt you may need a suede brush. After treating, spray on some suede protector. You can get this from a shoe-repair store.

539> You can get rid of water stains on suede shoes by wetting the entire outside of the shoe with water. Then, fill the shoe with newspaper and let them dry overnight. Use a suede brush to buff up.

540> Oil stains can be removed from suede with warm water and a nail brush.

541> Learn to do simple alterations, such as sewing on a button.

547> How to clean gold jewelry

Over time, gold jewelry can become tarnished and dull-looking. To give it new life and get it sparkling again, follow these easy steps:

1. Put a few drops of dishwashing liquid into some soda water.

2. Put your gold in a tea strainer and dip in for a few minutes.

3. Use a soft toothbrush to work the solution into the crevices of the jewelry.

4. Put the strainer under the tap and lightly rinse (put the plug in, just in case). Dry with a soft cloth.

542> Don't forget to take a picture of your dry-cleaning collection receipt with your phone in case you lose it.

543> Store jewelry in airtight bags to reduce any tarnishing.

544> A good way to select a dry cleaner is by their policy for lost or damaged clothing. You're probably willing to pay more to clean a suit you had to save up for.

545> Before dry-cleaning a garment, consider whether it's worth it. Remember, you can remove stains in other ways. Dry-cleaning too regularly will damage your clothes.

546> For men, appear more relaxed when tie-less but shirted by unbuttoning the second-to-top button.

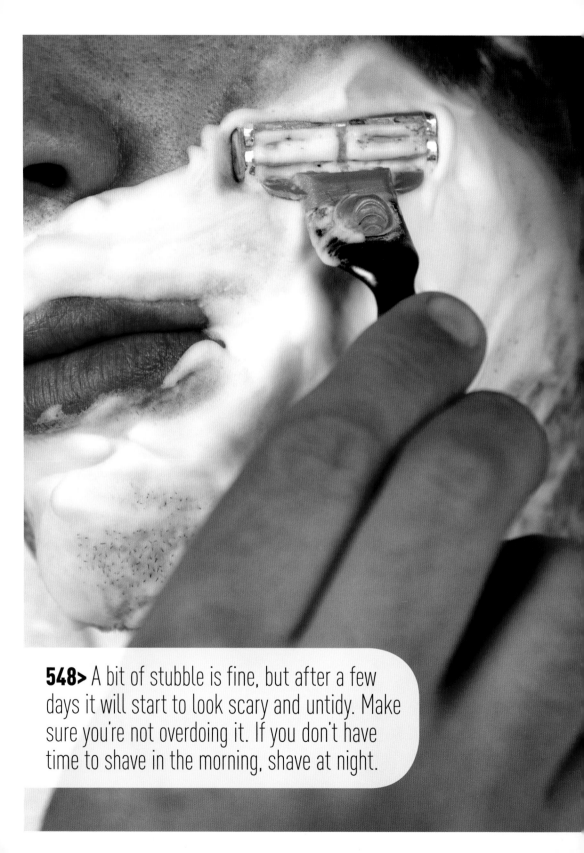

548> A bit of stubble is fine, but after a few days it will start to look scary and untidy. Make sure you're not overdoing it. If you don't have time to shave in the morning, shave at night.

549> Learn to buy clothes that fit you—many men get clothes that are too big.

550> Overdressing slightly is better than underdressing, as you can always take your jacket off.

551> Men often neglect their shoes. You don't need them to be pristine, but it's worth keeping them polished.

552> When you're buying a new coat or jacket, make sure it fits your shoulders 100 percent. You don't want to have to make alterations later on.

553> Don't forget to donate unwanted clothes. If thrift stores don't want them, large clothing stores and recycling centers have clothing banks.

554> If you need to cut down on the amount of clothes you have, think about whether you would buy particular items of clothing if you were shopping right now.

555> Don't try and wear too many colors. Three is about the limit to prevent looking garish.

556> Get to know what looks good on you and keep that style in mind. But don't be afraid to adapt it.

557> Why not match socks to another garment? Failing that, always opt for black socks unless you're wearing sneakers.

5

FOOD

558> How to dice an avocado

Avocados are delicious and very good for you—but they can often be difficult to cut up. Here, we show you a clever way of dicing an avocado, which takes the frustration out of the process. Simply follow these easy steps:

1. Cut the avocado in half lengthways using a sharp knife; separate the two halves.

2. Remove the stone—strike it with the knife, then twist it and gently pull it out.

3. Score each half with the sharp knife in a checkerboard pattern.

4. Finally, dip each half into a bowl of water to ease off the skin.

559> Need to keep salad fresh? Put it in a bag, blow into it, then seal it up.

560> Need to measure honey, peanut butter, or other sticky ingredients? Spray the measuring cup or scales tray with cooking spray. Because it's designed to prevent stuff sticking, your ingredient will slip out easily.

561> Need to drain spinach? Roll it up in a paper towel and shake.

562> Remember you can always add extra vegetables to salads and as accompaniments. You don't have to stick to the rules!

563> Why not match up vegetables to go with a meal based on common cooking times?

564> If you're adept with chopsticks, try eating a salad with them, rather than stabbing the veg with a fork.

565> If your bananas are close to being past their best, chop them into chunks (without the skin), place on baking paper, then freeze. Use them with custard for dessert, or for smoothies.

566> Dried beans and pulses are best, but sometimes you'll need to use kidney beans or similar from a can. Make sure you wash them first to remove excess salt.

567> Slice a bell pepper lengthways down one side, then keep cutting, rotating it until you have cut all the flesh off around the stalk.

568> Use a plastic shoe holder to organize food—put it on the back of a long cupboard door.

569> Want to ripen bananas quickly? Turn the oven on to 350°F (gas mark 4) and put the bananas in for five minutes.

570> Crushing garlic brings out the goodness—let it sit for a few minutes after crushing before you use it.

571> Clean any type of grinder by putting a spoonful of rice inside, grinding until it's a powder, then tapping it all out.

572> Got a seat warmer in your car? It's good for keeping a takeout warm.

573> Portion out snacks like nuts and pretzels so you don't eat too many!

574> Crack open walnuts by fitting two nuts together and pressing them together in your hand. Use your other hand to add extra pressure.

5 great ways to **eat better** at work

575> For a healthier breakfast at your desk, create a jar or container of healthy stuff, including a basic granola, adding fruits and berries on top.

576> Likewise, pre-portion nice salads to enjoy—make sure you put the dressing at the bottom and then mix it up when you want to use it.

577> Don't over-snack at your desk. It's hard, but take healthy snacks into work to compensate. Try and stick to regular meals. And especially don't skip breakfast!

578> They say to eat an apple a day—why not keep a bag of them in your desk drawer?

579> Dried fruit is a great work snack food.

580> Brown sugar is prone to going solid in the cupboard. Prevent this from happening by placing a marshmallow in a bag of brown sugar.

581> Got a serrated grapefruit spoon? You can use it to peel ginger (it follows the contours a lot better than a normal peeler).

582> Dish out condiments from a muffin/cupcake tin at a barbecue or family event.

583> To keep asparagus fresh, cut a little off the stalk and put it in a large jar along with a couple of inches of water. Cover the whole thing with a bag tied around the jar. Put in the fridge.

584> If you're going to be short on time to cook, prep vegetables in advance and store them in sealed containers in the fridge.

585> Put the unhealthy stuff at the back of the fridge. It may not help you (as you know where things are), but it will help other members of your family to eat more healthily.

KITCHEN HACKS

Cooking is part of our everyday lives, but you don't need to be a slave to your kitchen. Here, we show you how to be a more effective cook, with tips on preserving food and cleaning.

586>
Divide up meat before you freeze it

If you freeze meat, portion it before you freeze it, so you can break off the bits you need to defrost.

587> Problems removing the lid of a jar?

Use a spoon to press the lid upwards first to try and break the seal. Try at various points around the jar.

588>
Avoid saucepans from boiling over

A wooden spoon laid across a boiling saucepan really will stop it from boiling over.

589>
Revive old celery

You can re-crisp celery by cutting off the bottom and sticking it in a glass of cold water.

590> Stop your cutting board from slipping

If your cutting board slips but you need to do a lot of chopping, put a slightly damp dish towel under the board.

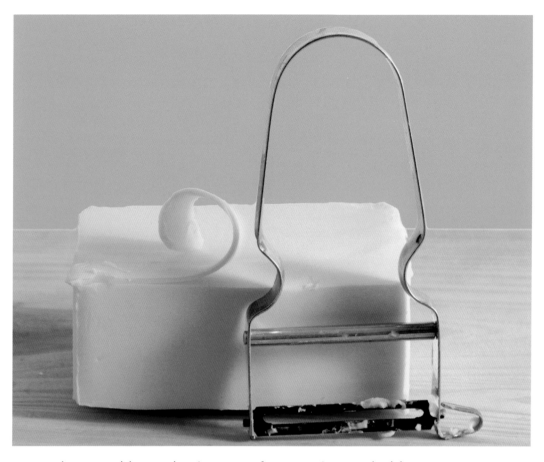

591> A vegetable peeler is great for creating curled butter. You can also make strips of cheese, too.

592> If you often can't remember whether you've already got enough of something when food shopping, take a picture of your fridge or main cupboard before you leave.

593> Store spices under a cabinet with a magnetic strip and some stick-on magnets.

594> Spice mixtures are expensive, so why not just make up your own? You can have fun experimenting, too.

595> If you season food with salt, consider using a little black pepper instead.

6 things you should know about **eggs**

596> Bad eggs float on the surface of water. You should throw them out. Fresh or nearly fresh eggs will stay on the bottom.

597> Is there a bit of eggshell you need to retrieve from the white or yolk? Wet your fingers before you delve in. If you don't want to use your fingers, try the neck of a plastic bottle.

598> Rather than crack eggs directly into boiling water to poach them, crack them individually into a small bowl and lower into the water. They'll hold their shape much better.

599> Use a muffin tin to make a batch of poached eggs all at once. Chuck them in the oven for 12-14 minutes at 350°F (gas mark 4), depending on how runny you like your yolk.

600> And, yes, you can even use an oven to hard-boil eggs. Just lie them in a muffin tin and put in the oven for around 30 minutes.

601> Egg boxes are great planters for mini herb gardens.

602> If you use a straw to drink a can of soda, put it through the ring pull to keep it from moving about.

603> Pierce a hole in your juice carton to stop it spilling everywhere when you open it.

604> You're removing the wine cork and it disintegrates into the wine. What do you do? Get a straw, that's what. Put the straw on top of the piece of the cork inside the bottle and place your finger on the other end of the straw to suck it up.

605> Need to chill a beer quickly? Wet a paper towel, wrap it round, and put it in the freezer. It will be ice cold in 10–15 minutes.

606> Tongs are useful for squeezing lemons if you don't have a squeezer to hand.

607> Frozen grapes are a great way to chill a glass of white wine without watering it down.

608> A cardboard tube, such as one used for savory snack packaging, is the best way to store spaghetti. You might want to cover the outside of the tube to avoid disappointment!

609> A fork is definitely the best way to shred cooked chicken.

610> Why not use drawer liners to brighten up your fridge, too?

611> If you can't face brown rice all the time, why not mix it with white rice? It doesn't have to be one or the other, though beware of different cooking times.

612> Make sure you're not cooking too much. If there's only two of you, don't cook for four! Divide the recipe up.

613> Use a cupcake case to catch drips from a flavored ice or ice cream on a stick. It looks a bit silly, but it works.

614> A spring-action ice-cream scoop isn't just great for ice cream; it's also a way to dish out a consistent amount of cake mix into a muffin tray.

615> Why not scoop out balls of watermelon? Use a small ice-cream scoop.

616> Last bit of chocolate spread stuck in the bottom of the jar? Why not put some ice cream in and enjoy your instant dessert?

617> Slice rock-solid ice cream using a hot knife.

10 top steps to eating more **healthily**

618> Fish is very good for you, so you should aim for at least a couple of portions per week (one of which should be oily). Salmon, for example, has plenty of omega-3 fatty acids.

619> Consider buying whole-grain bread instead of white—it is a lot better for you.

620> Likewise, you should look at whole-wheat pasta to get more fiber in your diet.

621> In the same way that you shouldn't overdo sugary sodas, don't overdo it with fruit juice.

622> Eat nuts! They have plenty of goodness, including fiber and vitamin E.

623> Why not substitute rice for some quinoa?

624> If you often eat too much, how about using a smaller plate? It really can work.

625> You can eliminate a lot of fat from your diet by cutting out processed sauces and dressings.

626> Eat more pulses, beans, and lentils—they're high in fiber and low in fat.

627> If you have trouble hitting your five-a-day, what about keeping a fruit bowl by the front door for when you walk out?

628> Blueberries not only add interest to bland cereal, they're also unbelievably rich in antioxidants, too, so add some to your breakfast.

629> You can remove the stem from a strawberry with a straw.

630> Likewise, you can pit cherries with a chopstick. Hold the cherry on the neck of an empty plastic bottle and press the chopstick down through it. The bottle will collect the stones.

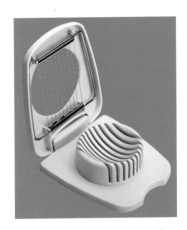

631> When buying canned fruit choose the ones with juice, not syrup.

632> You can use an egg slicer to cut strawberries— or slice mushrooms.

633> An aluminum tray is the best thing to defrost meat on, as it conducts heat.

634> For pancake mix, use a squeezable sauce bottle or jar so you don't end up dripping it everywhere.

635> You can make arty shapes using pancake mix—just use drips of mixture to make the outline of a shape and then fill in the middle. The outline will show as it will be browner than the middle.

636> Try making hash browns in a sandwich toaster or waffle maker—just fill it up with shredded potato, onions, and an egg.

637> Make unusual-shaped food with metal cookie cutters; they also make for interesting-shaped mini-pancakes (and fried eggs!).

638> Make plastic film wrap stick to a bowl by rubbing some water around the outside of the rim.

5 handy tips for **graters**

639> Use a Microplane® grater to grate garlic instead of chopping it. It's also best for zesting.

640> Clean a grater by grating big pieces of raw potato.

641> Cooking spray is also useful if you're grating cheese—spray the grater beforehand to make it easier.

642> Burnt some cookies? Use a smooth-sided grater to take off the charred bits.

643> If you have cold butter but need to spread it through a mixture, consider grating it.

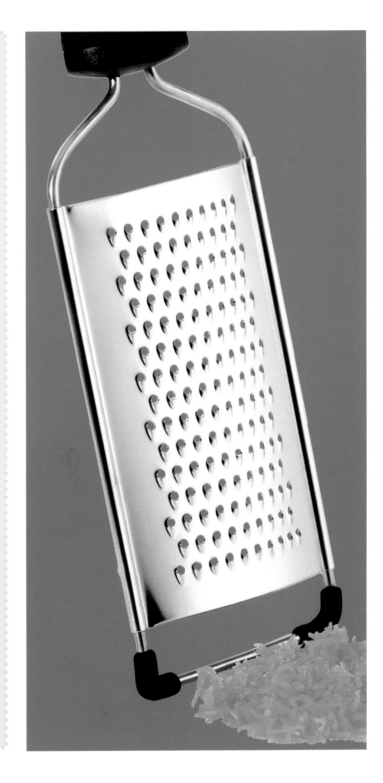

644> Bread gone stale? Make croutons instead. Simply cut into cubes, drizzle with a little olive oil or melted butter, then bake in the oven for 10 minutes or until brown.

645> Often have circular meats to put in a sandwich? Get better coverage by cutting two pieces in half and placing the flat edges against the sides of the bread.

646> If you want crispy bacon but don't have time to clean up after, make your own rack by folding heavy-duty aluminum foil into crinkles and putting it into your grill pan.

647> Need to toast just one side of the bread for a BLT or similar? Do it under the grill.

648> Get more ketchup in the small paper sauce container you get at fast-food outlets—just unroll the lip.

649> Soak wooden skewers in water so they don't burn in the oven.

650> Take calorie warnings about foods such as avocados with a pinch of salt. Remember that they add other nutrients to your diet.

651> Fold fully-open large snack bags inwards from the bottom corners so that they stand up and make a container for themselves.

652> Make a really sweet barbecue sauce by mixing a can of cola with ketchup, and brushing over ribs or chicken.

653> Baste a ham with cola as it cooks; the ham will be nice and moist, and the sugar will caramelize, too.

654> Dental floss is the best way to cut a cake horizontally into even layers. You can also use it for cheese if you don't have a cheese cutter to hand.

655> A Lazy Susan is a great way to decorate a round cake consistently.

656> Why not freeze portions of cookie dough?

657> Every time you go to fry something, ask yourself whether you could cook it another way.

658> Don't discard leftover boiled or roasted potatoes. Instead, chop into slices and fry them up the next day.

659> Why not prepare your own kebabs for a bit of a different dinner? You can use pretty much any meat or vegetable.

660> Freezing a premixed smoothie is a good way to save time in the mornings.

661> Drink plenty of water with your meal—it really will make you feel better.

662> Take a couple of liters to work with you each day, and aim to finish it by the time you get home, even if you drink most of it while commuting and at lunch!

663> Another tip is to keep a glass by your bedside so you can drink during the night if you wake, and in the morning.

664> You could also leave a glass by the bathroom sink and drink water after you brush your teeth.

665> If you take sugar in tea or coffee, cutting it out is a sure-fire way to reduce your sugar intake drastically. Can you cut down gradually?

666> Variety is the spice of life, but it's also the key to a healthy diet—write down what you eat across a week and consider what you're missing.

667> Coffee is rich in antioxidants, but, as with everything else, moderation is the key.

668> Pre-portion smoothie fruit so you don't blend too much in one go.

669> Green tea is rich in antioxidants—as is proper cocoa. Why not drink a cup?

6

FITNESS

671> After a run, get hold of some liquid as soon as you can. If you can't, consider alternatives, such as an apple or juicy fruit.

672> Like to eat? Try stopping when you are full rather than when your plate is empty!

673> Likewise, try and eat when you are hungry rather than absolutely starving. Being in the latter bracket encourages overeating.

670> Exercising in the heat? Consider rehydrating with a sports drink—the electrolytes will hydrate you faster.

674> Eat more slowly—you'll still get full and you'll eat less in general as a result. Plus, it's better for your digestion.

675> Think about taking a lightweight backpack on your run to carry water and some oat bars or chocolate for energy replacement.

676> If your run is over an hour long, then you need to think about your hydration strategy. Is there a shop en route where you can buy a drink, or will you take water with you? You don't need to drink as much as you lose, but you do need to be comfortable.

677> If you don't want to be going to the bathroom right before a morning race, only drink around half a liter of water beforehand.

678> Another idea: run a circular route so you can stop off for water at home or pass somewhere you could store a bottle.

679> Don't run immediately after a meal. You need a couple of hours first (though you might be able to get away with a little less of a break after a light meal).

6 simple steps to planning your **fitness**

680> If you struggle to keep yourself fit, set yourself some goals. It could be on a yearly (January 1?) basis or it could be week-by-week.

681> There are plenty of goal-tracking apps available for smartphones, some of which can remind you to exercise or go to the gym on a regular basis.

682> You could also write in your calendar what you plan to do on certain days of the week. Then, at the end of each week, refine the plan for next week based on what you did this week.

683> If you struggle with motivation, a personal trainer can really make the difference—not least because it will cost you money!

684> It's important to be realistic as well as aspirational. It's no good putting in your schedule that you will run five miles if you can't spare the right amount of time.

685> If you don't have an exercise plan and can't afford a personal trainer to create one for you, look online—there are plenty to choose from. Remember to refine it to suit you, though.

686> Set yourself the target of exercising three or four times a week. That way you're doing plenty, but not overdoing it either.

687> If you're starting off on the journey to fitness, remember that any amount of physical activity is going to be good for you. Don't be forced by others to do more than you feel comfortable with.

688> Make sure your training matches the goal you're working towards.

689> If you're a busy person, book runs into your schedule as calendar appointments.

690> Make sure you warm up for at least five minutes; 10 is better.

691> Ask friends to recommend a personal trainer. Although expensive, you'll get a program that's tailored for you.

692> If you're going on a big run tomorrow, make sure you're thinking about your hydration today. Ensure you're never thirsty, and cut down on alcohol and diuretics like caffeine.

693> Want to burn calories? Treadmills burn the most calories of all cardio equipment.

694> For a more intense workout, don't forget to adjust the incline as well as the speed. A varied program, where you change incline often, will burn more calories.

695> The same rules apply on the treadmill as when running in the street—make sure you warm up and take it easy to start with. And cool down, too, of course!

696> Interval workouts are also really good for burning calories and many treadmill programs can help with this. You can also find numerous programs online.

697> Wipe down any exercise equipment after you've used it.

698> Learn about the different equipment at the gym so you'll get to know how each will benefit you.

699> Try not to be on your phone while you're at the gym—view it as an extended screen break.

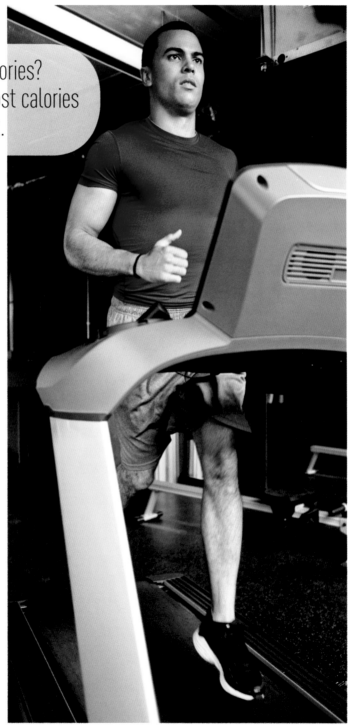

FITNESS HACKS

Whether you are new to exercise or have been training for years, these hacks will make your fitness regime run a lot smoother, whatever your choice of exercise.

701> Work out to music

An old-school music player like the iPod Shuffle is still best for exercise. It's small, unobtrusive, and inexpensive, and has good battery life as well as physical controls. It even has a clip for attaching it to your shorts or T-shirt.

700> Stock up on carbs

Carbohydrates should be a major part of your diet before a race—pasta is an obvious way to do this without resorting to sugar.

702> Hydrate while you run

You can get really good water bottles with handles you can hold while you run.

703> The life of running shoes

The shock absorbency of running shoes does wear out—but how quickly depends on how much you run. A good rule of thumb is to change them every 400 to 500 miles of use.

704> Freeze half-filled drink bottles on their side

Then, when you need to exercise, you can fill the other half of the bottle and have an instantly cold drink.

705> Don't be surprised that you run slower on windy days. Wind slows you down just like it slows down a car or plane.

706> Don't get sucked into doing a big run or other event if you're not up to it. It may be for a good cause, but it's a bad idea if you're not ready.

707> If you commute to work, then consider your lunchtime a haven. Remember to take as much of your lunch hour as possible—you need the break! You'll be more productive after a brisk walk.

708> Got an elevator at work? Don't take it. Walk up the stairs, though we'll let you off if it's more than 10 flights or if you're late for a meeting.

709> Often exercise in work breaks or at lunchtime? Keep a spare set of exercise clothing at work so you'll never be without.

710> Getting off the subway, tram, or bus a stop early in order to walk the rest of the way is a cliché, but it works.

711> Those looking to reduce weight should try to exercise for at least 30 minutes a day—that's the recommendation by the U.S. Department of Health and Human Services. Some other health services recommend that 45–60 minutes of activity has a better result because the body is burning plenty of fat by that point.

9 essential **running** tips for beginners

712> You'll soon get to know how long a run of a certain distance will take you, so you can time it with your lunch hour, or before or after work.

713> Even if you're a reasonably active person, don't dive into running several miles right away. Take your time to get into it. It's suggested to add no more than 10 percent to your weekly mileage.

714> Walk before you run. You should be able to walk for 30 minutes at a brisk pace before you can start running.

715> Cool down after running—remember the idea is to bring your heart rate gradually back to normal, so walk and stretch your leg muscles. Stretching is essential.

716> Don't think you can run in any old sneakers. You need decent running shoes. A specialist running store may charge more for the shoes, but it'll be worth it.

717> If you get embarrassed when starting to run, begin in a quiet place like a side street, riverside sidewalk, or grocery store parking lot, where there aren't too many people.

718> When you run, relax your arms and shoulders. Being tense will wear you out.

719> Don't clench your fists while running—you need to be relaxed.

720> Look ahead when running—not at your feet—to maintain good posture.

722> Stick to the food you know, especially around a race or competition.

723> If you're exercising within your capability, you should be able to talk (briefly, not necessarily all the time!) without getting out of breath because of it.

724> Providing you don't mind looking too silly, swinging your arms as you walk also burns more calories.

725> If you're trying to lose weight, stick to exercise where endurance is crucial—like cycling, swimming, running, or rowing.

721> If you're cycling, always keep pedaling, even on easy terrain—adjust your gear accordingly.

726> Had to take a break because of an injury or holiday? Don't do too much too soon. You don't want another injury (or get one for the first time) just because you had some time off.

727> You must have a snack after exercise—you need to replenish! But remember, it's not an excuse to spend the rest of the day packing away the calories, so look for a healthy alternative, such as fruit.

728> Varying the pace can have a good effect—as your body adjusts, more calories are burned.

729> A popular mantra for resting after a race is to take a day off for every mile you've run. It was first suggested by long-distance runner Jack Foster. However, you may find you need fewer rest days depending on your experience, or maybe you only need 10 days for a half marathon, for example.

730> If you're a regular walker, can you increase your pace from stroll to brisk?

731> In the winter it's not as easy to get out into the cold and exercise. Promise yourself a treat afterwards.

7 ways to have a more effective **swim**

732> Make your swim more effective—switch to an intensive swimming stroke for some of the time. Or could you go faster for one out of every three lengths?

733> If you're training for a running race, why not cross-train with swimming to improve all-round fitness?

734> Fit in a swim at the start, middle, or end of the day—you only need 30 minutes.

735> If you have a busy job, swimming at lunchtime can give you the peace you no doubt crave. Because you're away from your desk or other work, you really will get a break.

736> Putting a buoyant object between your legs— like a pull buoy—is a sure-fire way to get your arms working harder in the pool.

737> Swimming in colder water will burn more calories, as your body needs to work harder to keep warm.

738> You can do interval workouts in the pool. Look online, where you'll find plenty of programs.

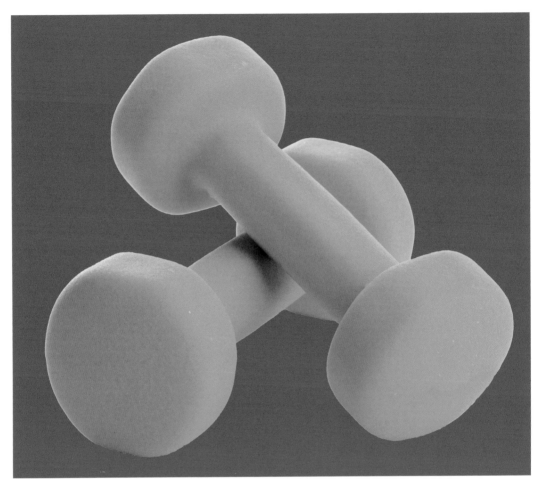

739> Why not add some light weight training to your plan? It's best to start slowly with just a few exercises.

740> If you're new at the gym, ask yourself which equipment you'd like to use. If it's the exercise bike, all well and good.

741> During training periods, rest days are important. Make sure you get a break from exercise.

742> If you're having a go at weight training, try a variety of exercises that target all the body's major muscle groups.

743> Don't be a gym hog! If you're in a smaller gym and there's someone waiting to use the same equipment, be mindful of the time.

744> Choose a gym first by location, then price. Your gym must be convenient for home or work. If it isn't, you won't go so often.

745> A gym buddy (it could be your partner) could be the key to making you attend the gym regularly.

10 essential tips for **stopping** smoking

746> If you're looking to stop smoking, you need a powerful reason to quit—otherwise you'll end up starting again. So find it!

747> Stress is the main reason many people smoke; so find some other way to relieve it. Think about when stress is an issue. Is it work-related, or are there other stresses in your life?

748> If you go back to smoking temporarily, assess where you went wrong before trying to give up again. Try to think about how good you felt physically once you'd given up.

749> Are there particular situations that encourage you to light up? Perhaps you have a cigarette after a particular meal or when you drink alcohol, for example. Think about the steps you can take to avoid these situations.

750> There will be times when you'll crave a cigarette, so what can you do for those few minutes? Is it a case of taking out your phone to text someone, or perhaps making an effort to start a conversation at that point?

751> If you have a relapse and regret it, set a new date in your calendar to give up once again.

752> Can you replace smoking with something else—like a new hobby?

753> The most important thing is to think positively. Remember PMA— positive mental attitude. It really does help.

754> Don't go cold turkey— there are plenty of ways to cut down your reliance on nicotine without suddenly starving your body of it.

755> Consider avoiding situations where your smoke-free self could be tempted to light up again, such as taking a break with a smoker at work.

756> Joining a sports club is a good way to get fit. You'll also meet lots of other people.

757> If you want to try yoga, there are plenty of websites with free classes to watch. You can also access sites like www.yogatoday.com that offer daily yoga classes for a monthly subscription.

758> If you're training at home, try to have an area just for your fitness kit. If you have to get your stuff out each time, you're more likely to "forget" to do it.

759> Always buy the right exercise ball for your height.

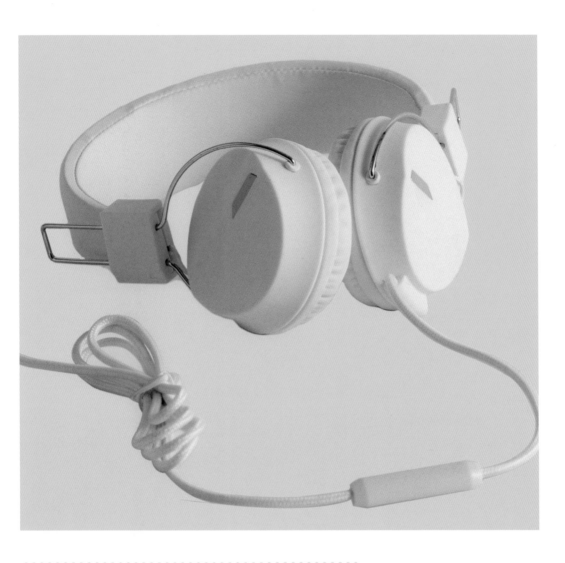

760> Download music or podcasts to your phone or music player beforehand, so you're not fiddling around too much when you actually get to the gym.

761> For headphones, we recommend getting specialist fitness headphones with ear pads that can be washed. You can use normal headsets and headphones, but they may not stay in your ear so well, and might get a little sweaty!

762> If you're training, plan extra sleep, as you'll need more energy.

763> If you have a family and want to get them more active, find somewhere you can visit where you have to walk around. If you decide to go to the zoo, choose one in a rural location that's more spread out.

764> Staying fit means nothing without enough sleep. Too little sleep won't help your body. Some studies have shown that not getting enough sleep can actually increase the possibility of weight gain.

765> Once you've tried everything out, you may be more comfortable with some gym equipment than others. Get a feel for what suits you.

766> Keeping a training diary—or even a blog—can force you to keep up your fitness regime.

767> If you fancy getting to a military level of fitness, the UK Army has a fitness app available for iOS and Android.

768> If you're going to run a marathon, you should be able to do a 20-mile run beforehand.

769> Why not mix up your exercise for further motivation? If you regularly train at the gym but it's a little tedious, how about going swimming or running with a friend one day a week?

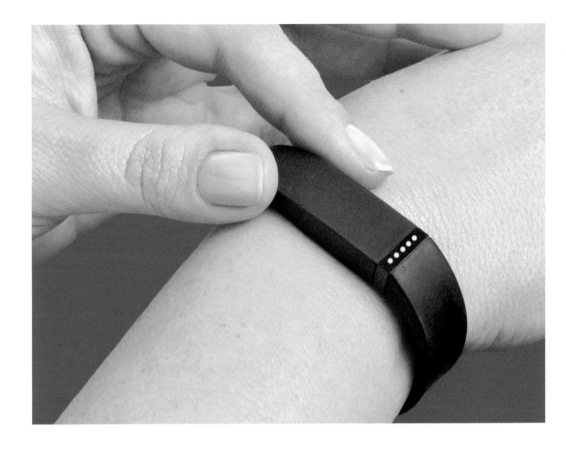

770> One of the key things about getting fit is that you should enjoy it. If you're not enjoying it, ask yourself why. Do you need to try something else?

771> You do, however, need to stick with it for at least a few weeks before you can really say: "I don't like this." If you decide to give up, ask yourself why, and then find another activity.

772> If you're bored by just running, why not try triathlon training? Even if you're not initially tempted by a race, it adds huge variety to your regular workouts because of the different lengths of exercise for three different sports.

773> Walking tours are fun, as there's entertainment while you walk.

774> People walk an average of 4,000 steps per day. Consider targeting significantly more than this by using a pedometer.

775> Don't feel you have to aim high immediately. Gradually increase the amount you walk each day. Pedometers and fitness tracking devices are great for this, as are smartphone apps like Apple Health and Google Fit.

5 tips for a **great** sleep

776> Bright lights are a no-no before sleep because it disrupts the production of melatonin. Make sure you take time to relax before turning in for the night.

777> If you simply must work late, you need a break before going to bed. The ideal wind-down time is two hours, but if this is not possible, try and do something to relax, like reading a book.

778> It's been shown in various studies that teenagers have problems falling asleep if they use gadgets in the last hour before bed. Perhaps you could implement a tech curfew an hour after dinner?

779> The best thing is to remove temptation and not have your phone or tablet in the bedroom at all. Should upstairs be a phone-free zone?

780> If you need your phone with you, consider setting it to Airplane Mode at night. Alternatively, consider investing in a normal alarm clock, so you're not tempted by your device.

7

TRAVEL

781> Stay in a lot of hotels? Remember your room number by taking a photo on your phone. Alternatively, dial the room number into your phone, call it, and immediately cancel the call so the number is saved in your recently dialed list.

782> Many hotels don't have tea- and coffee-making facilities in the room. Consider this when booking if it's important.

783> Take the shampoo from hotels. These small containers usually fit within the 3.4 ounce liquid restrictions.

784> Often stay in bad hotel rooms? Get a tumble-dryer sheet and tape it over the air conditioning for a better-smelling room.

785> Ask for the business card of the hotel or hostel where you're staying, and keep it in your pocket so you can always get back. Or use the wallet your hotel keycard comes in.

786> Worried about pickpockets opening a bag? Use a safety pin to secure the zipper.

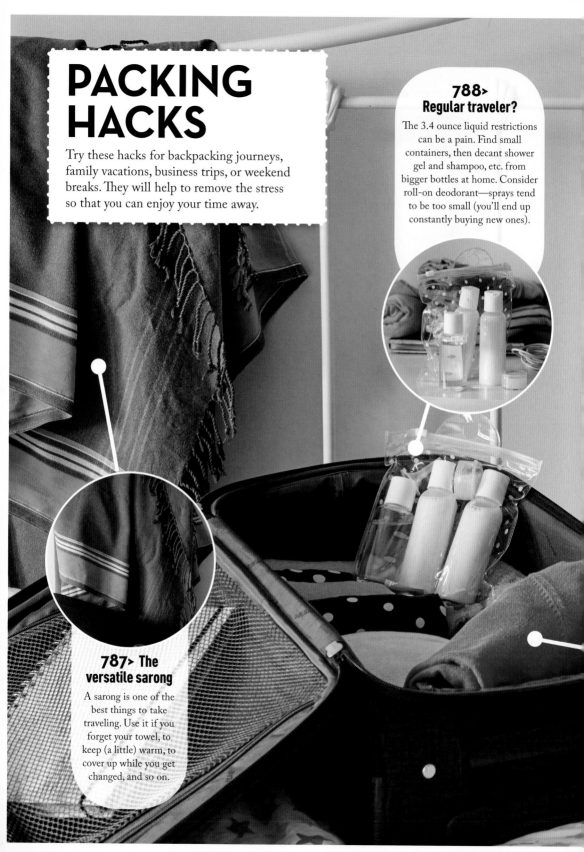

PACKING HACKS

Try these hacks for backpacking journeys, family vacations, business trips, or weekend breaks. They will help to remove the stress so that you can enjoy your time away.

788> Regular traveler?

The 3.4 ounce liquid restrictions can be a pain. Find small containers, then decant shower gel and shampoo, etc. from bigger bottles at home. Consider roll-on deodorant—sprays tend to be too small (you'll end up constantly buying new ones).

787> The versatile sarong

A sarong is one of the best things to take traveling. Use it if you forget your towel, to keep (a little) warm, to cover up while you get changed, and so on.

789> Always pack earplugs

You will need them as protection from fellow travelers, traffic noise, babies on planes, and much more. If you're staying in any kind of shared accommodation, you'll be thankful for them.

790> Stay untangled

A pencil case or glasses pouch is a great way to store charging cables when traveling.

791> Pack efficiently

Traveling a lot will help hone your packing skills. Rolling your clothes is an especially efficient way to pack.

792> Meeting local people is great, and even if you don't speak the language, hand gestures go a long way! Smiling also gets you places. Chances are, the locals will be very welcoming and you won't regret the effort you made.

793> See fewer places to enjoy yourself more. It can be tempting to cram a lot in, but often it just doesn't work.

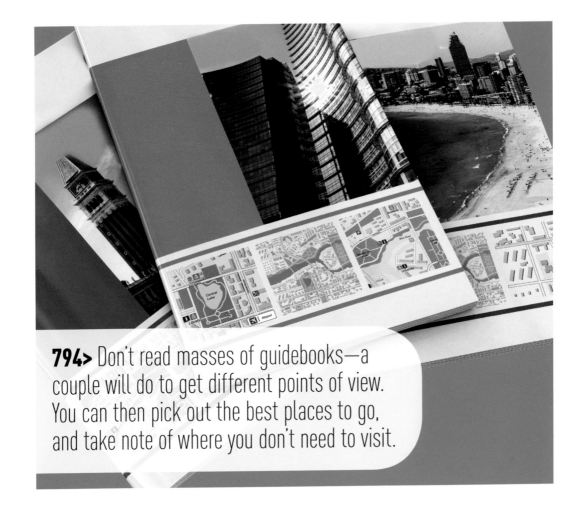

794> Don't read masses of guidebooks—a couple will do to get different points of view. You can then pick out the best places to go, and take note of where you don't need to visit.

795> Check out other people's experiences online, whether that's through feedback on sites like Airbnb or TripAdvisor, or anecdotal evidence on Twitter.

796> Also remember to take reviews with a pinch of salt. People don't like to pick fault after they've met face-to-face, while if there are 10 positive TripAdvisor reviews and one really negative one, it's likely to be a one-off rather than a systematic failing.

797> Find free places to stay at www.couchsurfing.com (though don't expect hotel-standard luxury!). Staying with a local is often the best way to put yourself out there and really get to know a place.

798> If you need to wash clothes when traveling, hang them up to dry with safety pins.

799> Keep scented soap in the same compartment as your dirty clothes to keep your clothes smelling clean.

800> Take the least stuff you can get away with if you're backpacking. After all, you will be carrying it ALL.

801> Traveling often means there will be times when you're in high spirits. That's cool, but if you're on your own in a strange culture, you need to have a certain self-preservation instinct. Stay in control.

802> If you're backpacking, it's good to keep a diary of your experiences. While you've got photos of people you met and places you visited, chances are you won't remember the conversations you had or some of the experiences you shared.

803> Mark your baggage with a piece of tape so you always know it's yours. This is especially the case if you're away on a short trip with a basic wheeled bag—a lot of them look VERY similar!

16 ways to have a better **flight**

804> Remember that non-stop is always better than direct (direct flights may stop off).

805> When you buy your plane ticket, make sure the name matches your passport EXACTLY.

806> Regular travelers always carry wipes with them to clean tray tables and arm rests.

807> Night moisturizer is the best thing to rub into your skin for a long-haul flight.

808> If it's a long-haul flight, consider paying to select your seat (if that is your only option). It can make the difference between a good flight and a bad one.

809> Couples may find it's worth paying to prebook seats in advance to avoid being seated separately on the plane.

810> Drink lots of water. When you're offered a drink, ask for water in addition to whatever else you want, and don't be afraid to ask for refills. Long-haul galleys often have water jugs available.

811> Always take snacks with you for the flight. A lot of airlines aren't that great for light eats, especially on long-haul flights where meals are often served after take-off and before landing—there's quite a gap in between!

812> Breathe in vapors from any hot drinks through your nose, as the dry air in a plane stops it from working properly. If you're unwell, bring a flask with lemon, and get it filled with hot water.

813> Bring a sweater even if it's the height of summer. Chances are you'll wear one if it's an early flight, as it will be cold.

814> Actually, take the clothes thing a step further—take a change of clothes in your cabin baggage. That way, long delays and baggage losses will seem like an inconvenience rather than the end of the world.

815> Don't put your coat or jacket in the locker—use it as a makeshift blanket (alternatively, bring an actual blanket!).

816> Don't forget to wear your heaviest shoes and your biggest coat on the plane.

817> You might want to take a picture of your baggage so it can be easily identified if it gets lost. This is especially useful if you take a lot of flights and always use the same bag.

818> Flight socks are essential for comfortable long-haul flights—they'll keep your feet warm, too.

819> If you fly a lot, invest in an amazing pair of sound-canceling headphones. You won't regret it. Even if you don't want to use them for music or in-flight entertainment all the time, they'll make your long-haul sleeps a lot more peaceful.

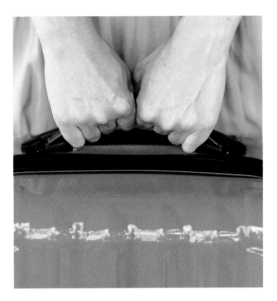

820> Traveling alone? Make sure you can handle your baggage by yourself. Don't expect someone else to be on hand to help.

821> If you have a bit of time in a place and a reasonable sense of direction, why not just start walking to explore? It's always good to have a map (even if it's on your phone) as backup.

822> If you have allergies or other medical information, make sure you keep a card in your wallet explaining them.

823> If you're a regular traveler (or just go away most weekends), always have a toiletry bag ready to go, complete with toothbrush. You're minimizing the chance of forgetting anything.

824> Taste the local food wherever you go. Even if you don't end up enjoying it, it's great that you've tried it. Exercise some caution, though—a market stall with a long queue is a lot better than one without!

8 golden rules for using the **internet** on vacation

825> Checking work emails on vacation is an absolute no-no. If you're tempted, think about how you can relax instead.

826> Social networks can make our minds very busy and aren't conducive to relaxation. Consider turning off Wi-Fi or cellular data to avoid updates.

827> Alternatively, turn off push notifications altogether, so your smartphone won't alert you while you're trying to relax. It's worth disabling your work email temporarily or—if you may be tempted to enable it—remove the account completely and just add it again when you get home.

828> If you want to use the internet in another country, always check what packages your cell phone network has to avoid expensive roaming charges. You'll probably be able to pay for a certain amount of data per day.

829> Getting ahead on work messages on the last day of your vacation sounds like a great idea, but it's counterproductive as you will fret about going back to work. You can guarantee something will have happened that you didn't want to know about!

830> Going traveling for a while? It may be better to use a different SIM card or rely on data rather than calls—after all, you can Skype and text with WhatsApp; neither of which uses the cellular network.

831> If you've changed your cell phone or contract since you last used your phone overseas—or are using it overseas for the first time—make sure your network operator has removed international call barring on your account.

832> Avoid social networks when on vacation— especially if people have a habit of posting things about your work.

833> Check out the local customs and culture. Falling foul of these could cause you a problem or—worst-case scenario—time in prison. If you meet another traveler who has been somewhere longer than you, find out from them what's acceptable.

834> When backpacking, it's best not to take yourself too seriously. Relax and try not to worry about what others think about you.

835> Backpacking? Don't plan everything—the whole idea is that you're making it up as you go along. Picking an end travel date is, of course, understandable, but just earmark a few things you'd like to do, rather than form a completely defined plan for what you will be doing on, say, Wednesday week.

836> If you're staying places where a top-notch smartphone will be a bit showy, consider buying a cheap cell phone just to keep in text contact. Keep your smartphone in your baggage and use it privately.

837> If you need to attend an important event when you're traveling, consider putting your pristine items in individual freezer bags. This will stop them getting crumpled.

838> If your journey is complicated, or you're away traveling for weeks at a time, expect things to go wrong. They will. If you're the kind of person that doesn't like it when plans change, have a backup plan so you don't worry.

839> Trust your instincts—if a situation doesn't feel right, do what you feel. But don't be scared of new places—this is what you've come to experience!

840> Don't make assumptions about other travelers—chances are you'll be wrong.

841> If you're backpacking and meet someone you get on with, consider changing your plans to hang out with them.

842> Often leave the house and fret you haven't locked the door? Do something unusual to remember you've done it: dial a number on your phone, or put the key in a different pocket.

843> Tours are a great way to meet fellow travelers—and that's as true if you're 20 and backpacking in Southeast Asia, or you're 65 on an island tour of Sardinia.

844> If you want somebody to travel with, ask people. Don't wait for others to make the, ahem, first move.

845> Cash is everything. Don't expect to pay with credit or debit cards unless you're going to big cities. If you get there and can use your card, then great, but you need to take cash with you.

846> Stash your cash in different places. Some in your hotel room—not hostels unless you have a locker—some in your bag or a sock, and some in your wallet. You'll protect yourself against the loss of your bag or wallet if you do this.

847> Take an empty water bottle through airport security and refill it after.

848> A small bottle or plastic storage box is a good jewelry container.

849> Think about volunteering. It's a great way to meet new people and do something worthwhile. You'll also learn a lot about the culture and people that you visit.

850> If you're away for a long time, you'll no doubt want to do things as cheaply as possible. But keep an eye out for opportunities where you can stay somewhere a lot nicer for just a bit more money; or perhaps a deal at a nice restaurant. You'll really appreciate it.

851> Alone at the bar and need to go to the restroom? Put a beer mat over the top of your drink. It means you're coming back.

852> Wind is often an issue when camping—especially if you're cooking outside. A windbreak is handy in these situations.

853> Problems sharing an air bed when camping? Get two air beds instead. You'll have a much better night's sleep.

854> Invest in a good foot pump for camping. You won't regret it.

855> Always have spare tent pegs in your tent bag.

856> Need to light a fire but don't have any kindling? Use tortilla chips or a similar snack.

16 tips to deal with **work trips**

857> If you have a busy schedule while you're away, run through it a couple of days beforehand, and talk it over with the colleagues you're going with. You can deal with any timing issues then, rather than haphazardly on the trip.

858> Indeed, it can be healthy to agree on a "work curfew" time, after which you no longer talk about work or answer emails.

859> Traveling with someone on the plane? Don't insist on sitting beside them and check in online by yourself. You can't get away with this for loved ones, however!

860> Don't be bullied into doing things you don't want to (like staying out late) when you're away for work. They don't own you. Although this might not be so easy if you're entertaining clients.

861> If alcohol is involved and you're expected to join in (and want to), always make sure you haven't had as much as the others. If you're getting tipsy, that's the time to stop. Keep hydrated.

862> You don't have to always dress smartly, but make sure you take the right things. A T-shirt and shorts won't give the right impression unless you're going to the hotel gym or you have a leisure day.

863> Don't expect colleagues to be constantly working when they're away for work. They probably want some down time. And that may mean they don't want to hang out with you.

864> Likewise, you shouldn't be working all evening and into the night on work trips. Sometimes it's necessary, but you need a break.

865> Always keep the conversation respectable. If you don't know the colleagues you're away with that well, don't talk about anything you wouldn't want your boss to know.

866> If your trip involves an onerous dinner or social occasion with clients, put it in perspective—you're going out somewhere nice (probably) that your work will pay for, so focus on choosing yourself some good food and enjoying the wine.

867> Use a work trip as an opportunity to get to know your colleagues better.

868> Ensure where you're going to be working has internet access if you need it, whether that's in your hotel room, at a client's premises, or elsewhere.

869> Unless you have someone whose job it is to sort the logistics, stay in charge of your hotel bookings, transfers, boarding passes, and so on. Do you need to book restaurants?

870> If your trip is more than a couple of days, take an evening for yourself if you don't have to meet clients— maybe go to a movie theater, or if you're staying in a city, go and visit a landmark.

871> If you have to share a room with a colleague you don't know that well, the bathroom is your sanctuary. Change in there (but don't hog it) and keep your stuff tidy in the room.

872> Chances are you'll be staying in separate rooms or even separate hotels to your colleague(s). Learn how to keep in touch with them—are they email reliant or do they text a lot?

873> Take versatile clothing items at all times. Try not to take outfits you can only wear for a particular occasion (unless, of course, you do actually need them for a particular occasion).

874> Keep an open mind when traveling—you never know when an opportunity might present itself (perhaps someone will ask or offer), or when you might be forced to do something different through circumstance.

875> Mark your bag as "fragile" for better handling. You can abuse this too much, though—your bag needs to be a decent size to try it!

876> Buy a battery pack for your phone that's small enough to carry in your day bag. You don't ever want to be without power.

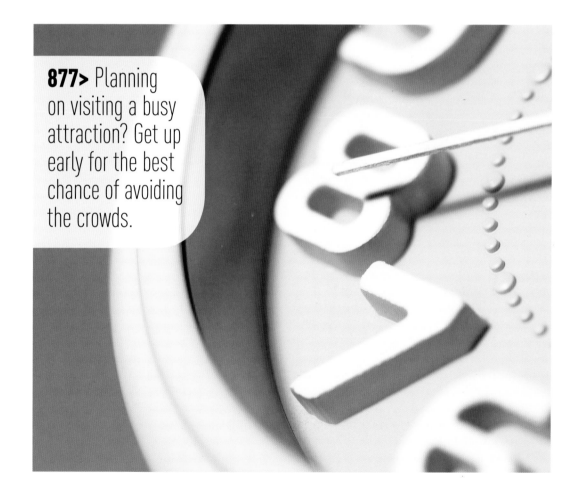

877> Planning on visiting a busy attraction? Get up early for the best chance of avoiding the crowds.

878> Make sure you always have at least six months on your passport and at least two blank pages.

879> Keep digital copies of all your documents on a laptop or USB drive. That's your passport, birth certificate, insurance documents, and important phone numbers. Back it all up onto an external drive and ideally into the cloud as well. In addition, carry photocopies of your passport with you.

880> If there's someone you know who has been to a place you're going, it's worth picking their brains, even if you haven't been in touch for a while. They'll be glad to help.

881> Allocate time to travel between places in cities.

882> Set calendar reminders for when your visa or passport runs out—even if it's many years in the future.

883> If your long-haul trip is less than a few days, is it possible to time eating and sleeping on your home time zone to minimize the effect of jet lag? This technique is often used by racing drivers and sports teams.

884> If you're in a new place, why not kick back for a while outside a local café (or by the window in a bar), and check out local life? This is as good in a city as it is in a small village.

885> Melatonin can work for fighting jet lag.

886> Change your watch to your destination time as soon as you get on the plane. Then behave as though you are in the new time zone; providing you aren't ravenous, don't bother with meals that are at totally the wrong time.

887> Try to get a normal night's sleep when you reach your destination. You must get at least four hours' sleep, known as "anchor sleep."

888> An empty lip balm or lipstick can make a great money bill holder.

889> Sending photos to family and friends can be a great idea to keep in touch. You may not call for weeks, but you can still give them a good flavor of what you're up to.

890> Take lots of photos while traveling (and if you don't want to, why not?). Phones are great for snapping pictures, of course, but you may want to take a cheap digital camera as an alternative. Make sure you take time to enjoy what you're photographing, though— don't just take pictures!

891> Just as you should protect yourself against the potential loss of a wallet or bag, you should be totally prepared to lose your laptop, tablet, or phone. Make sure you don't have copies of anything on any device that you don't have elsewhere.

8

KIDS AND PARENTING

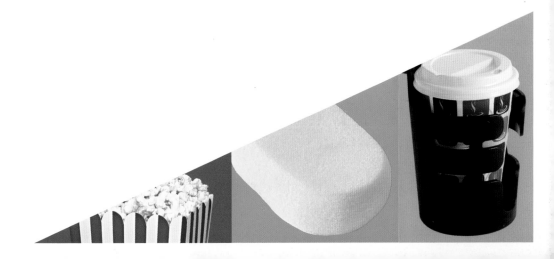

892> Birthing classes can be a great way to meet people, but they also mean you compare pregnancies, child development, and much more. It's hard, but try to rise above it.

893> Take a baby first-aid course when your first-born arrives—you won't regret it.

894> In the initial days as a new parent, remember that you're in the same boat as billions of others. You will feel like you're not a good parent. You are—just keep going.

895> If you're a new parent, be prepared to try new things. Go to groups with similar-aged children.

896> Put babies on their front a few times during the day. Baby gyms are great for this.

897> New parent or parent-to-be? Don't take the advice of other parents too seriously. Remember, above all else, that you'll have your own style.

898> If you don't have a baby monitor, but are staying someplace where you need one, use your and your partner's cell phones. Make sure you have plenty of minutes, or if you have plenty of data on both devices, call over Skype or WhatsApp. Put the phone that's with you on speakerphone.

899> If your baby wails when you leave the room, try leaving a muslin or soft toy with them that smells of you.

900> Dad and baby/pre-schooler groups can be a really great bonding time. They're also good for the dad to meet other like-minded guys they can talk through parenting woes with (and then go to a bar with later).

901> If you're entitled to paternity leave, take all of it. You won't regret it. Take more time if you can, but schedule any other leave for days when your partner won't have as much support (say, after the grandparents have left).

902> Consider saying no to new responsibilities, whether it's at work, a community organization like a church, or a weekly sports commitment. We all need balance in our lives, but your kids need you as well. Plus you don't want to risk burning out.

903> Don't be afraid of that parent and toddler showing at the local movie theater. You might really enjoy it!

904> Get an extra laundry basket for stuff that must be done in the next load. That way the kids won't be without their soccer kit, and you won't be without the only long-sleeved shirt you have for your toddler.

905> Don't potty-train too soon. Wait until your child senses they're about to go and asks for diaper changes.

906> Get a plastic hook and hang bibs on the back of the high chair.

907> If you're a new dad, prioritize your workload. You'll never get the chance to bond with your newborn baby again.

908> Nearly new sales are great places to buy baby gear. So is eBay. Don't be afraid of used goods. You think your child cares? Think again. You think your baby will be in that coat for more than five minutes? Think again.

909> Keep an extra set of clothes in the locker at daycare or school.

910> Persevere with food. If children don't like food you cook, you may need to try it again and again.

911> If you work from home, you'll need to establish boundaries—and preferably a closed door—between your child and your work. You can't have them running in all the time.

912> Don't get into the habit of pandering to whims (and offering up bad foods you know they'll gobble up instantly) if they don't eat. You'll wear yourself out.

913> If your child starts throwing food because they're no longer hungry, just take the plate away.

914> Instead of blowing relentlessly on food to cool it down, get clever with cold water. Float that bowl of porridge in a little bowl of water for rapid cooling.

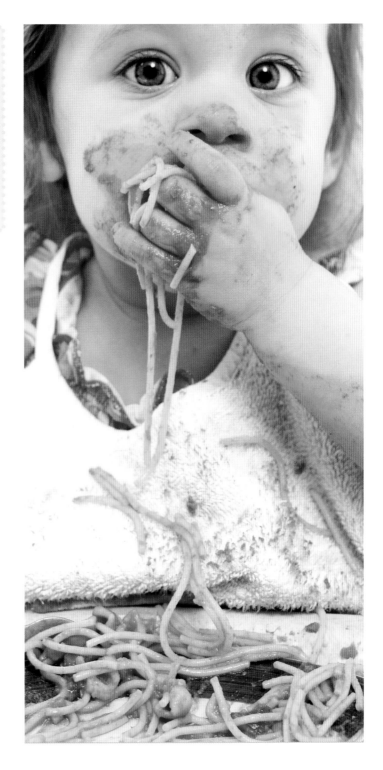

KIDS' ROOM HACKS

Bring some order to your child's bedroom by trying out some of these hacks. Get your child involved, too, so that they can learn how to look after their toys and keep their bedroom tidy.

915> Pre-loved books

Kids don't need new books and really don't care if something was published in 1976. Thrift stores are great places to pick up well-loved books. Or do you know someone with books in their attic?

916>
Get musical

Basic musical instruments can be a great way to get kids to join in with the music they hear. Encourage them!

917>
Imaginative storage ideas

Wire baskets make great wall-mounted toy organizers.

918> Stop kids falling out of bed

A swimming pool noodle can be handy to prevent kids from falling out of bed—put it under a fitted sheet.

919> Get kids to clean their rooms

Encourage your toddler to put away their toys. Although frustrating at first, it will save you hassle in the long term.

920> Need extra storage for kids' books? Get some fixtures that will go on the back of a door.

921> A frozen sponge makes a great ice pack for little injuries.

922> Accept that your kids will hurt themselves—toddlers have minor scrapes all the time. Don't blame yourself or your partner (this doesn't excuse neglect, of course).

923> Reinforce boundaries using positive language. If they're rude or hurt you physically, explain what they did wrong.

924> If your child angers you, say, "You have made Daddy very sad; are you sorry?" or similar. By being consistent with this, you'll make them say sorry (even if they can't talk yet and just give you a hug).

925> Subtly let child carers know how you expect them to reinforce your parenting principles. If you had to tell your child off for throwing, relay the tale to the other carer in a light-hearted fashion, so they know how to deal with the same situation.

926> Encourage your toddler to walk rather than go in their stroller as soon as they can—it will prevent the stroller becoming the default option rather than getting the exercise they need!

927> If you make a threat, always follow through on it. Don't let them see weakness!

928> If you do something wrong, apologize to your child. It'll teach them to do the same.

929> Praising your children is good for their wellbeing, but you should always seek to establish boundaries.

930> Increase a child's understanding by explaining what you're doing: "We're going to Grandma's this afternoon," or "After breakfast we'll go to the shops," will go a long way.

931> Pick your battles, whatever age your child is. Try not to focus on every little thing they're doing wrong. They're just being a child.

932> Try and find more encouraging ways to say things that don't involve "no" or "don't." No can become an automatic word, so encourage them to do something else instead.

933> Even if you don't agree with what your partner has told your child, it's best to go along with it for consistency and then discuss it afterwards for next time.

934> Ask your child for their opinion. Or ask them what they did today when you get home from work. Engage them in conversation (even if they can't talk yet!).

935> Make eye contact with your child as much as possible to reinforce your bond.

936> If you and your partner often buy coffee, get a cup holder for your stroller. You can't push a stroller (that well) with one hand.

937> Soft toys are lovely, but they can get everywhere. Store them in a laundry basket or, alternatively, use Velcro® strips to attach them to the inside of a cupboard door or shelf.

938> Is your baby or toddler attracted to one toy, blanket, or teddy bear more than any other? Make sure you buy a replacement that's exactly the same in case of loss.

939> For long journeys—such as on a plane—take toys that have been hidden away for a while.

940> Need to wash building bricks? Get a net and do it all in one go.

941> Read at least one book together with your child every day from early on—you can start when they're newborn, as they love the sound of your voice. Just before bed is the ideal time.

942> Store a mini-library of books in the back of the car seat in front of your toddler. Let them choose the book they want to read at the start of the journey. This won't be so good if they get motion sickness, but it's worth a go.

943> Play classical music as you get your baby or toddler ready for bed—it can have a nicely calming effect.

944> Reinforce the idea of being a good person using the characters in the books you read to your child.

945> Take time to listen to your kids when you ask how their day was. If they seem particularly downcast, try and get to the source of the problem before it becomes a bigger issue.

946> Have a family meal each day—with young kids this may only be at weekends because of early mealtimes. And sit at the table to have it.

947> Know there's usually something behind a tantrum. Is it hunger? Tiredness? Mostly it will be the latter.

948> Take it in turns to choose the food for your weekly family time, too.

949> Make a barrier for toddlers out of polyvinyl chloride (PVC) piping and four corner joints. Then cover the construction with material or stretched plastic.

950> Don't put your baby/toddler/child into bed asleep—they need to learn to fall asleep themselves. Tell them a story, put them down, and let them drop off.

951> Putting your child in their own room after a few months may seem early, but you'll all get much better sleep as a result.

952> Establish a ritual for bedtime as early as possible, and evolve it as time goes on. It'll be something they come to depend on.

953> Equally, don't be afraid to make exceptions. Still at a family party when it's nearly bedtime? Don't fret—providing they are OK, of course.

954> Public tantrums can be awkward, but sometimes you've just got to ride them out. After the child has calmed down, ask them what would make them feel better.

12 ways parents
with **teenagers**
can make life easier

955> If your teenager wants a particularly expensive phone, consider whether it's worth buying it outright for a birthday or Christmas present, and then having it on pay-as-you-go, which you can give them a monthly sub to top up.

956> Show them that last year's iPhone really isn't that much worse, despite being significantly cheaper.

957> If you regularly pay your teenager's cell phone bill despite high call costs or extra data, think about whether you should stop doing it and just pay a set amount to them instead.

958> Get to know your teenager's friends' parents—it helps to be able to check things or discuss any challenging situations, even if it's just a school project they're all struggling with. You can also see through any tales of the "I was at Paul's house doing an assignment" type.

959> Sharing your own mistakes can make teenagers see they shouldn't fall into the same trap.

960> Encourage them to get a job when the time is right. If they can learn about the process of earning and spending their own money now, they're less likely to waste money in the future.

961> Give kids an allowance and don't bend on giving them more—you want to teach them how to budget. If they overspend, not being able to go to the shops after school teaches them a good lesson.

962> Get them to open a savings account, even if they're just saving to buy Christmas presents for family.

963> If you want to take your teenager's money-management skills further, give them a monthly budget for their school lunch.

964> You need to choose your moments to talk to teenagers about money. A great opportunity is when they need something, like a new bicycle or driving lessons.

965> Establish ground rules. Make it clear that the penalty for breaking them (such as being out beyond an agreed curfew) will result in them being grounded. Stick to your promise of punishment.

966> Learn to strike a balance between interest and prying. It's hard and you won't always get the balance right, but accept you won't know everything.

967> A first payslip is a good opportunity to talk to teenagers about tax. A lot of adults have major problems understanding tax, so give them a head start!

968> Set aside quality time to spend with your child. Turn the TV off and let them choose an activity if they're older, or get them playing if they're younger.

969> When they're old enough, create a sheet of basic rules for watching TV and other screen time (such as gaming).

970> If you need to distract your kids, listening to music, looking at books, or experiencing age-appropriate audio books are all great ways to avert focus from the TV. Or what about the radio?

971> Having friends around can be a bit of a drag for a parent, but tell yourself that those friendships will likely last.

972> Reward good behavior and completed chores with an incentive, such as a treat on a Saturday.

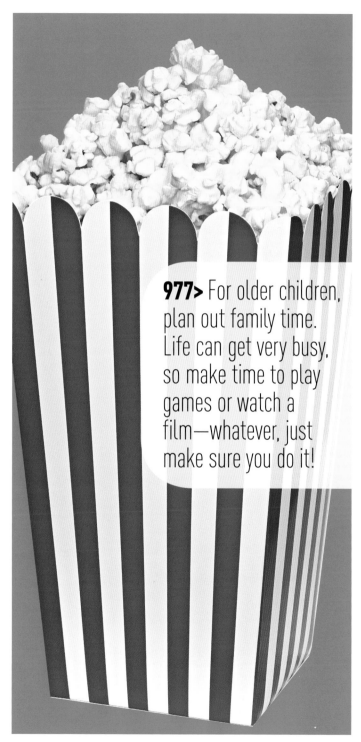

973> Making older children and teenagers do chores isn't draconian. It makes sure they're involved in the household and know what responsibility is.

974> Suggest your kids invite their friends around. If they don't want to, it's time to explore why.

975> If your child wants a TV in their room, tell them no and give them a time slot on the main TV.

976> If you turn up at home to find an extra child there, explain to your child that you'd like to know next time—even if they just send you a text to warn you.

977> For older children, plan out family time. Life can get very busy, so make time to play games or watch a film—whatever, just make sure you do it!

15 essential tips to manage **kids and tech**

978> It's easier said than done, but you need to be aware of what apps and games your child is accessing. Instigate parental controls on any computing or tablet devices they're using.

979> Keep family mealtimes and gatherings tech-free. Teach your kids that this is valuable time and nobody should be on phones, games, tablets, or laptops.

980> Make sure you are not "doing as I say, not as I do" when it comes to electronic devices, whatever age your kids are. Try not to use your phone or tablet at home while your kids are around. If you're a stay-at-home parent this is easier said than done, so it's all about proportion—10 minutes on Facebook while your kids want to play isn't OK; replying to a text is fine.

981> Don't give your child your password. They should have their own user account, which you can then manage and modify privileges for as they get older. Even if they use the same PC, you don't want children anywhere near your stuff and doubly so if you have photos, household spreadsheets, or work documents around.

982> If your children are using your PC, it's time to back up anything important (you should be doing this anyway, of course).

983> You should always passcode-protect your own devices.

984> Don't lock everything down—it's good for the child to feel like they're free, even if they're not. Let them download free apps rated appropriately for their age, for example.

985> Small kids are drawn to phones and tablets. Save yourself a lot of bother (and some tantrums) by using your device sparingly and preventing it from becoming something they simply have to have.

986> Family Sharing on Apple devices also enables you to easily share your calendars and photos, and you can use the Find My Friends app to see where your children's devices are.

987> If you have a problem with children surreptitiously using electronic devices in their rooms, schedule your Wi-Fi so that it turns off at night—you can do this in your router's settings. Of course, you need to do this in such a way that doesn't cause problems for you. If you use something like Netflix on your TV, use a cable to connect your TV to the router—that way the wired connections won't turn off even if the Wi-Fi does.

988> If your family has Apple devices, set up the Family Sharing feature. It enables your children to ask you if they can purchase something from iTunes or the App Store. The purchases are then deducted from your card. You can also set up the service so you're asked if they can download free apps, too.

989> Most young people don't realize that almost everything you do online can be tracked. Tell them this using the example of Google selling targeted advertising. Don't scare them, though!

990> Do warn kids that posting too much about themselves can come back to haunt them later in life, especially on public networks like Instagram or Twitter, or public posts on Facebook.

991> Beware of in-app purchases. There are so many free apps and games out there it's really not necessary for (especially younger) children to buy apps, games, and in-app features.

992> Some internet providers offer their own parental control service, which can block unsavory websites, or individual websites you specifically don't want accessed.

993> Tell your kids not to say anything to others that they wouldn't want to be told themselves. Hurtful texts and social messages have a habit of coming back to bite.

994> Family day? Suggest activities your kids might like to do and let them be free to decide.

995> Don't put your personal preferences in the way of your children doing sport. If you like baseball but they prefer soccer, take comfort from the fact they are getting physical exercise.

996> Help your kids to view online relationships with friends as an extension of their offline friendships, not a replacement for them.

997> Ideally, you should be friends with your teenagers on Facebook. If this isn't possible, you can watch their public page for any misdemeanors (this is a good opportunity to talk to them about privacy settings if you, as a non-friend, can see posts they shouldn't be sharing publicly).

998> Give yourself a break. Make an event of getting takeout or going to a café for food to give yourself a night off cooking.

999> It can be difficult for kids to prioritize in the early teenage years. Help them see what's important—that doesn't always mean that schoolwork is top of the list; it could be that they want to get into the soccer team, and so they need to make time for training.

1,000> Parenting is hard. Schedule a date night for you and your partner once a month, even if you just watch a film together at home.

Index

Acknowledgments

Thank you to my wife, Leila, for her patience and support, as well as everyone at Quintet — both in and out-of-house — for their help and guidance.

Dan Grabham is a U.K.-based writer, specializing in technology and lifestyle. He is currently editor of tech website T3.com, formally edited Lifehacker UK, and was part of the team that launched TechRadar.com. His interests lie in sport, technology, and music, and he enjoys outdoor activities, including hiking and running. Dan lives and works in Bath, U.K., with his wife and young son. Visit his website: dangrabham.com, and follow him at twitter.com/dangrabham.

Image credits

Alamy: Mint Images Limited 86

Getty: Celia Peterson 244

iStock: hocus-focus 26; gotvideo 28; ShotShare 36; bill oxford 39; Educester 47; AndrejaBudjevac 48; 4x6 49; mediaphotos 54; kokouu 59; Boris Yankov 60; Ferran Traite Soler 61; andresr 64; Christopher Stokey 76; ThamKC 77; Pixsooz 78; PLAINVIEW 79; Konstik 80; warongdech 84; ozgurkeser 85; APCortizasJr 90; Robert Simon 90; Adam Gryko 91; Serg Myshkovsky 92-3; Created_by_light 95; YolandaVanNiekerk 96; pumpuija 100; bjones27 101; Christian Nasca 102; siraanamwong 104; psvrusso 106; Don Nichols 107; Sasa Radovic 110; v_zaitsev 113; galbiati 114; Zoran Kolundzija 114; Lars Koch 115; gbrundin 118; pidjoe 119; powerofforever 122; Ivan Bliznetsov 124; Franc PodgorAlek 126; EsHanPhot 127; Lee Rogers 131; Maxal Tamor 132; Aleksandar Milutinovic 137; YinYang 140; artwell 141; kkgas 142; LouisHiemstra 147; matka_Wariatka 150; ValentynVolkov 155; Tatiana Fuentes 157; DNY59 159; darjeelingsue 160; Haber_1965 161; Thomas Perkins 162; Peng Li 162; Leonid Shcheglov 163; BlackAngus 164; Burwell and Burwell Photography 166; zi3000 167; OlgaMiltsova 168; SusanneB 168; AngiePhotos 169; Joe_Potato 172; Malcolm Nigel Carse 175; shapecharge 177; OJO_Images 180; &#169KRUS 185; BraunS 189; Imgorthand 194; Igor Stepovik 208; User2547783c_812 214; Kuzmichstudio 217; quavondo 218; Janka Dharmasena 220; Dmitry Chulov 221; franckreporter 223; deucee_ 226; DNY59 228; isabelle Limbach 229; Vinicius Ramalh Tupinamba 238; michaelpuche 241; Paul Johnson 245; skynesher 248

Shutterstock: Bloomua 18, 21, 246, 249; Andrey_Popov 19; Alexander Supertramp 24; tanuha2001 25; Yoana Genova 30; shipfactory 31; Yeamake 37, 46; Canadapanda 38; omihay 42; Sergey Nivens 45; matka_Wariatka 51; Alexey Boldin 53; bikeriderlondon 55; Micolas 56; qvist 57; Stasique 58; donatas1205 67; Coprid 67; Waleri Warkentin 71; triocean 72; kurhan 80; Geo-grafika 87; MAHATHIR MOHD YASIN 95; Anteromite 98; Robyn Mackenzie 99; Lane V. Erickson 105; asharkyu 111; gualtiero boffi 112; Marina Lohrbach 115; SunCity 117, 136; nito 125; gvictoria 130; Anna Vishnevskaya 134; Denis Filatov 138; Africa Studio 139, 143, 181, 205; Photographee. eu 141; forestpath 155; sacura 171, 188; Kenishirotie 171, 183; lzf 173, 174; Subbotina Anna 176; Dudarev Mikhail 182; Blazej Lyjak 184; EpicStockMedia 186-7; Stepan Kapl 190; Sakarin Sawasdinaka 191; koya979 192; Stephen VanHorn 196; wavebreakmedia 197, 239; Sukpaiboonwat 200; ProStockStudio 204; Maxx-Studio 204; Drue T. Overby 209; Efired 210; c sa bum 211; Julia Lototskaya 212; rvlsoft 213; Wara1982 215; Diego Cervo 219; nikkos 227; Mariusz S. Jurgielewicz 234; Vadim Georgiev 240; Aaron Amat 242; Milan Ilic Photographer 243; Monkey Business Images 247; Brian A Jackson 250; Alexander Mak 251

While every effort has been made to credit photographers, Quintet Publishing would like to apologize should there have been any omissions or errors, and would be pleased to make the appropriate correction for future editions of the book.

All trademarks, trade names, and other product designations referred to herein are the property of their respective owners and are used solely for identification purposes. This book is a publication of The Quarto Group and has not been licensed, approved, sponsored, or endorsed by any other person or entity. The publisher is not associated with any product, service, or vendor mentioned in this book, and does not endorse the products or services of any vendor mentioned in this book.